HOW TO BE A DIGITAL REVOLUTIONARY

BY VIOLET BLUE

DIGITA PUBLICATIONS

DigitaPub.com

Published in the United States by Digita Publications, San Francisco, California, DigitaPub.com.

Cover design: Violet Blue®
Artwork based on works by artists Natalia Hubbert and Seita, licensed through Shutterstock.
"How To Be A Digital Revolutionary" font: Hussar Woodtype, free for commercial use.
Text design: Violet Blue®
Logo art: Violet Blue®
First Edition
ISBN: 9781521338285
10 9 8 7 6 5 4 3 2 1

.

TABLE OF CONTENTS

Low-cost protective gear

Know your rights; if you're arrested

When you can't be there: digital support

CHAPTER 10: RESOURCES

CHAPTER 11: THE DIGITAL REVOLUTIONARY PROJECT GUIDE

AFTERWORD: ACKNOWLEDGEMENTS

ABOUT THE AUTHOR

INTRODUCTION
RISE

One of the most popular American myths that followed me out of childhood to come back for a body-slam in my adulthood was the one about how anyone can be President of the United States. Even a woman.

I'd already realized most facets of the American Dream mythology were lies. We most certainly are not all equal in the American systems and institutions, nor any political or justice system, and certain people have an investment in keeping it that way. It didn't take long for me to figure that out as a young woman living on the streets as a teen, seeing and experiencing police brutality, and later trying to get a fair shake in writing and journalism, while men helped other men copy my work and congratulate their successes. But part of me still dreamed that a woman could be president.

The ubiquity of myths like these—of fairness and right rules and justice for all—reminds me that time does not, in fact, heal all wounds. It shows us that these harmful myths fester as power is abused, and abused some more, until suddenly we're all living in a rupture. It shows us that racist bullies will gorge themselves on power; that history is ignored at everyone's peril; that science is in a constant fight to prevent a slide into the next Dark Age. It shows us that corruption loves company.

You don't need me to give you a laundry list of the very real and imminent dangers of a Trump presidency, any more than you need me to point to any of the despotic regimes Trump adores. You don't need me to list the attacks on people of color, women, and LGBT people already enacted by the new president and his administration. Nor do you need a righteous rant about political leaders who betray national values, or about the despicably greedy Internet companies that are their tools and handmaids. I also don't need to tell you that our problems won't be resolved when he's gone; the symptom reveals the extent of the infection.

We know why we're here.

The difference between last year and this year is that the people exploiting and abusing our civil rights and assaulting our privacy no longer seem to even bother pretending to be good.

As a society, we may be fractured, but we are re-forming into something that's a bitter pill for fascists to swallow. No wonder they're trying to parade in the streets; not just emboldened by the trends in American leadership, but genuinely threatened by having to live in a world where they're surrounded by facts and the power of diversity. The truth is scary—and they should be terrified, for we who resist are a credible threat. It is the zeitgeist we live in. I think it's no coincidence that many of the biggest films and shows whose worlds we escaped to after the 2016 election were about revolutions and rebellions. Ones led by women, people of color, fighting against fascism and authoritarian regimes. Into a future free from at least the bigger tyranny, if not the selfish, shortsighted bastards who sold everyone out for a brass ring.

That is the spirit of this book. *How To Be A Digital Revolutionary* illuminates why we're here and what we can do. It looks at actions we can take right now, standing in this moment with devices in hand, as both eyewitnesses and active participants to significant social change. This book is woven from clear explanations about murky topics like surveillance and censorship, hands-on strategies to dial back news-overwhelm and rage-fatigue, first-person accounts in hacking, practical safety advice for protests, and gritty reporting on rights abuses in the digital realm.

This book runs down the hazards of taking action to fight injustice and fascism in the digital age, providing you with a roadmap for effective resistance. A small consciousness shift begins in Chapter 1, "Resist," where I explain why we all need to think like hackers now—and how to do it. Life in a surveillance state requires we re-calibrate our relationships with tech and each other, and here we'll also explore the practicalities surrounding our love/hate relationship with anonymity. You'll also find out how and why you should focus your fight, because we never feel like we're doing enough, and ways you can resist every day.

We must not be outraged into inaction. The constant bad news, the anger we feel every day, and the stress of feeling helpless are making us feel crazy. It doesn't help that trolls are weaponized, or that bots are political—when they used to just push penis pills and SEO. Chapter 2 is "Self-Care Rules Everything Around Me (SCREAM)". It was created with the help of psychologists, and it explains how you can establish a baseline on your news and social media consumption, advice on overwhelm and anger, and how to reduce the onslaught of troubling information with automated tools that let you control your information input so it works for you. This chapter also goes in-depth on dealing with poison people who try to hijack your cause.

The mess of modern security makes us feel like securing ourselves is a losing battle, so why try? As it turns out, there are simple things anyone can do that get you out of the target zone. Chapter 3, "Hack-proof your life," walks you through getting your security together in easy steps, and shows you how to take the first steps to push back on surveillance. This chapter also includes getting your personal info offline so when the trolls come they have nothing to "dox" you with.

"Your Phone Is a Tracking Device" is both the name of Chapter 4 and an undeniable fact. This chapter explains how your phone can be a danger that, with help, can be understood and mitigated. Authorities, advertisers, idiot app makers, and greed obsessed companies like Facebook all have a stake in tracking and selling us without our knowledge—yet leaving our phones at home during a march or protest isn't an option for anyone. As I explain, there are simple tricks you can do to get surveillance stakeholders off your back. In this chapter you'll learn how to make your phone work for you at marches and protests, all about circumventing phone signal interception, and everything you ever wanted to know about "burner" phones.

Just like a carbon footprint, everyone has a surveillance footprint. Identifying, reducing that footprint, and working at getting it to zero is what you'll find spelled out in Chapter 5, "Defy Surveillance." You'll discover that powerful security tools, formerly only used by hackers and techies, have become readily available and extremely easy to use. Find out what to use, how to use it, and everything you need to keep your communication private, encrypted, and secure. You'll also get honest advice on choosing and using encrypted apps.

Welcome to modern tech: It's shoddy, it never works right (or it crashes and may blow up), it sells us out to anyone who asks … And yet it's the sword with which we've become a credible threat to corrupt politicians and civil rights attacks like state-sponsored censorship. In Chapter 6 ("Gear Up") you'll find out how to make your tech work for *you*, and not its makers. This chapter tells you how to put together a simple, yet edgy, digital revolutionary toolkit from what you already have—or get advice on buying or making new gadgets. Learn to make a "burner" phone, a little portable anonymity filter for Internet browsing ("Tor in a box"). Find out how to build a portable free Wi-Fi library for documents and resources to share with your group, or create a glowing open source protest sign that will call 911 or your lawyer if confiscated. This chapter also delves into avoiding bad security and activist advice, and lists a few security gadgets you absolutely need.

Censorship is how powerful entities assert their control, hostility, and indifference over our struggle for civil and human rights. In Chapter 7, "Fight Censorship," learn the different kinds of censorship that's used on us, how that censorship is implemented, and how to circumvent it with security tools and tweaks as simple as changing a few app settings. Censorship is also used as an attack tool on social media by trolls and political pawns who want to silence women, LGBT people, and people of color. And they often get away with it under the soft oppression of algorithms and broken "report abuse" functions. Find out how to fight back and be heard, no matter what. And if you have something to "leak" to the press or other organizations, this chapter also covers tools and safety for whistleblowers of all kinds.

As protests are formed online, memes rally people to unity, and calls to action are broadcast on social media, being heard is critical for any cause. In "The Revolution Will Be Shared" (Chapter 8) learn how to make sure your media gets seen, how to track response to it, and how to make memes that matter. Learn how to use live video in situations both ordinary and extreme. Find out what you must consider when you livestream anything, from public marches to episodes of police brutality. When you work so hard and take risks to have your media seen and heard, you need to know how to measure its impact. Here, discover ways to measure, quantify and refine your sharing, and stay sane with automated tools that do the tracking of topics and events for you.

As things that were never thought possible become the new status quo, it's blowing the minds of many that marches calling for revolution fill our streets. Daily calls for action on social media have become "clicktivism" that actually works, and we now know that showing up makes a difference. Chapter 9 is quite literally about "Taking it to the Streets." However, showing up can put us at risk. This chapter tells you how to organize, plan, march, and protest safely, from items and resources to bring with you, to prepping your devices for a protest. You'll find out about safety plans, buddy systems, phone issues, what to wear, and more. Learn how to prep for protests that may become violent, and what to do if things go wrong and you deal with police. Since not everyone can be mobile or available, this chapter also covers being an off-site support team when you can't be there in person.

Go deeper in the "Resources" chapter, or dig into the DIY gadget creation in the "Digital Revolutionary Project Guide," both of which are at the end of this book. Everything mentioned in every chapter, including tools, tutorials, links, books, and groups are collected and expanded in "Resources." Seriously: That chapter has as many rabbit holes as you have the time to investigate all the goodies I've planted there. The open source "Project Guide" lists all the DIY gadgets mentioned throughout this book, with links to tutorials and even explainers on basics (like soldering) to get beginners started. Finally, the "Acknowledgements" section thanks the people and communities that are in this book, and who made it possible.

In a time of rampant injustices, I hope that *How To Be A Digital Revolutionary* offers us a powerful new handbook for the resistance, and a way forward for change.

Violet Blue
San Francisco

CHAPTER 1
RESIST

The election of Donald Trump in 2016 is when millions of American citizens realized how urgent it is to fight for democracy—and they did it with smartphones in hand. People around the world began identifying with what is being called "The Resistance": A growing progressive movement to confront a presidency that seemed shamelessly determined to disempower, dehumanize and oppress many if not most of its citizens.

This wasn't the first time the U.S. saw its citizens take to the streets to fight injustice: We've marched for suffrage and civil rights, and against the wars in Vietnam and the Persian Gulf. The AIDS Coalition to Unleash Power (ACT UP), which formed to defy the U.S. government's indifference to the AIDS crisis, may have been the first movement that showed a thoroughgoing willingness to document itself as it happened. Participants deliberately brought video cameras to both meetings and protests to tell the story not being told by press. But the 2017 election wasn't even the first time we spread our message with livestreaming and status updates. That big moment may belong to the citizens of Ferguson, Missouri, in the wake of Michael Brown's 2014 death at the hands of police.

Nonetheless, we were a little behind compared to some other countries, like Tunisia, Libya, Egypt and Yemen, whose Arab Spring drove their governments out of power. But we made up for it with numbers.

The day after Donald J. Trump was sworn in as president, the United States saw its largest day of protests in its entire history: The 2017 Women's March. On January 21, somewhere between 3.3 and 4.6 million people—more than one in 100 Americans—took to the streets.

The Women's March was a global event with sister marches everywhere from Antarctica to Paris, all to oppose Trump's inauguration and stand up for women's rights. These events were organized almost entirely online and through smartphone apps. The people created their own media coverage—in fact, they were their own coverage. Their experiences at the marches were streamed, Tweeted, posted about on Facebook, and more. Media outlets played catch-up with attendees, with headlines in every major news outlet relating not what had happened, but what marchers were sharing. In this age of "post-truth," this was one place where facts couldn't be faked and signs couldn't be censored, because the people's media had become the story. News sources were left reporting what people had reported.

Prior to that, just two weeks after the 2016 election, a church in the Boston suburb of Brookline embraced encrypted communications–from the pulpit! The Unitarian Universalists at First Parish decided to answer hatred with love. The new U.S. government had embraced a harsh anti-immigrant and anti-Muslim stance right out of the gate. Every day brought news of anti-immigrant threats from the government as well as violence or hate crimes perpetrated by racists emboldened by the regime change. First Parish put a plan in motion to become a sanctuary for undocumented immigrants just after the election.

In church that weekend, Reverend Rebecca Bryan told her parishioners about "WhatsApp," a communication tool she thought they should adopt. WhatsApp, she explained, is where they should communicate via a "a group that is entirely encrypted, where we know what we share is completely safe." What Bryan suggested, and First Parish's status as a sanctuary, marked the beginnings of a modern Underground Railroad, where targeted immigrants could find help from the church, in secret, outside the prying eyes of authorities.

It didn't take long for the nightmare of official rhetoric and unofficial violence to become State-sponsored reality. Trump signed the first of his anti-immigration and anti-refugee Executive Orders almost immediately after the election, and enacted new deportation rules in February. With these moves, the federal government was granted full force to find, arrest and deport those in the country illegally, regardless of whether they have committed serious crimes. Lists were made. People were–and are still being–rounded up in raids; refugees were and are forced to flee the United States to Canada–many to avoid being deported to their country of origin, where they might end up dead. Families were (and are still being) ripped apart.

Hundreds of thousands of protestors have fought for the human rights and civil liberties of those targeted, and much of that fight has been when digital revolutionaries show up and take a stand. But more needs to happen to protect our immigrants. What we learned from Trump's quick action is that he really does intend to make life hell for America's immigrants. We really do need an underground railroad in the 21st century.

That such a thing would be possible, let alone a necessary, is a shocking idea for some Americans—and a new idea for many young citizens. But it might not be so shocking for those whose families were rounded up and placed in internment camps in California, Idaho, Utah, Arizona, Wyoming, Colorado, and Arkansas during the 1940s. Nor did it seem to as shocking to those whose ancestors who were forcibly removed from West Africa hundreds of years ago and brought to this country as slaves. It probably doesn't shock those who can track their descent from the original inhabitants of North America, who were murdered and displaced in the name of Manifest Destiny. Those are just a few of the things in U.S. history that must never be repeated; unfortunately, there's plenty of room for more, and our country isn't the only one that seems determined to produce as many such atrocities as possible during our lifetimes.

The 2016 Women's March may have been the biggest breakthrough for the digital revolution, but again, it is in no way the first. The killings of Trayvon Martin in Florida in 2012 and Michael Brown in 2014 in Ferguson, Missouri, sparked demands for justice that galvanized a new wave of civil-rights activism, driven by young people of color taking advantage of digital media.

When it was time to march, protest, and get into the fray to demand change, groups like the Black Youth Project 100, the Dream Defenders and the Million Hoodies Movement for Justice were ready. Their significant online followings and willingness to engage online and off put fuel in the fire of media attention, and ensured that their stories were told.

Digital revolutionaries have been hard at work for years, working for human rights, fighting tyranny and censorship, and pushing for positive social change since the Internet got into the hands of at-risk populations decades ago. But we didn't really have a clear picture of what that looked like until the Arab Spring; a series of anti-government protests, uprisings, and rebellions spread across the Middle East in early 2011.

The goal of these citizen-led events, organized through social networking sites, was to bring political reform and social justice. With apps, posts, shares, live video and photos, Twitter blasts and more, the digital revolutionaries helped to bring global awareness to injustices, affected governmental change, helped fellow civilians to be aware of the underground communities that exist, and to find others willing to listen and help.

"We use Facebook to schedule the protests" an Arab Spring activist from Egypt told the press, "and [we use] Twitter to coordinate, and YouTube to tell the world."

By picking up this book, you are a digital revolutionary. You join the ranks of people using tech to fight for democracy, equality, freedom, speech, and human rights—from Women's March attendees and immigration airport protesters to Arab Spring participants and those who put their lives on the line in Ferguson.

This book is an arsenal of tips, tools, ninja moves, recipes, insider information, support systems, and roadmaps for the digital revolutionary. This includes anyone who wants to know how to better protect their digital privacy and security while making a difference. It warmly welcomes tech newbies and the digitally savvy alike. It gives you a range of tech tools to choose from so you can resist injustice, censorship, and discrimination at exactly the level that's right for you.

This book is also for the person who just wants to learn about a cause without everyone knowing about it. Or they want to make sure they don't get hacked or spied on at a march or rally. You might want to make memes that matter for good causes. Or maybe you'd like to help others working toward change, or need a little support when you feel overwhelmed by all the wrongs that need righting—there are tools for emotional and social support in these pages, too.

Perhaps you keep hearing about encryption and want to stand up for privacy by using it, but don't know where to start. Maybe you're genuinely worried about a "Big Brother" scenario coming true. It could be that you picked up this book because you feel compelled to do something for the resistance every day, and you're wondering if clicking "like" or "share" really matters. You might also be someone who wants to up their game with sharing live video and photos, to make sure the real story gets told.

This book is a digital guide for everyone who wants to make change in the world. It'll tell you how to easily and seamlessly use an encrypted app to chat about private stuff, and guide you through circumventing censorship when people try to control what you say, see and hear online. You'll also learn how to attend an event without risking your digital security or privacy (and how to get things securely online while you're there). To get you started, here are nine principles of being a digital revolutionary—the fundamentals of this book:

- Resist.

- Adopt new technologies.
- Reject surveillance.
- Take back your privacy (with security).
- Get involved.
- Teach others.
- Think like a hacker.
- Disrupt "Big Brother".
- Demand change.

Think like a hacker

Throughout this book, I'm encouraging you to think like a hacker. That means you'll take technology that's meant for one thing, and shape it for another, better use. You might combine technologies to make an electronic protest sign that's controlled by multiple people. Or maybe you'll figure out how a hacker might attack you, so that your online opponents can't "dox" you (expose your private information). Hacking might mean finding a way to better distribute your message across different social media platforms, or helping others to use encrypted communications. Hacking, whether it's technology, society or life, is at the center of this book's message.

Being a digital revolutionary, whether you do it a little or a lot, means you're tapping into a rich and storied history of people living in the digital underground. I'm not necessarily talking about the kind of protests seen in the Arab Spring, or pitching in with a railroad to help immigrants to safety. The digital underground is at least four decades old, with roots in hacking and information security communities worldwide.

The people who create apps like Signal, Disconnect, and

WhatsApp come from hacking's rich history. People who have hacked and worked in InfoSec (information security), but who have always believed that privacy is just as important as security. People whose trust doesn't come easily, and have seen power misused for negative ends. Also, people who want to work to make the world a more secure place,

Hackers are the original digital revolutionaries, using technology to be heard about dangers when authorities are wont to ignore them. German hacking organization Chaos Computer Club, founded in 1981, became famous in 1984 when it discovered a serious flaw in German banking computer network Bildschirmtext and reported it to the bank–but was ignored. To make its point, the group transferred money to itself and notified press that it had done so. CCC transferred the money back in front of press the next day. Like the American hacking group L0pht (1992), CCC positioned itself as a source of public information about the security failures in the new online world.

For telling governments about security problems, hackers have been lumped together with criminals, hunted down and arrested. The U.S. government's sweeping country-wide raids and crackdown on hackers in 1990, called Operation Sundevil, became the inciting incident in the founding of the Electronic Frontier Foundation (EFF) by three hackers with the goal of defending speech and civil liberties in cyberspace–by defending the rights of hackers and hacking.

Like the digital revolutionaries taking to the streets today, hacker culture is global and extremely diverse in age, race, gender, sexual orientation, religion, politics, and much more. It is this diversity that gives hacking's most notorious factions, hacktivists, their ethos and celebration of outsider culture. Hacking culture tends to have a strong sense of justice, a desire to right wrongs in systems that have become corrupt, dated, harmful, or otherwise broken and harmful to at-risk individuals.

Life in a surveillance state

Our world is more connected than ever. As a result, we're spied on and tracked by both companies and our government, well beyond our consent. Thanks to this spying and tracking, our digital security is a terrifying mess. Our personal records are constantly being leaked, while at the same time we're being censored online. When we set up an account on social media, email, or anywhere else, many of us probably don't realize we agree to bizarre TOS (terms of service) that means our privacy can be violated in any way a company wants.

On one hand, being connected is giving us leverage and power as citizens. On the other, it's being used against us. Surveillance and data collection go hand-in-hand. Social media and advertising companies are continually compiling big data dossiers on us, trying to match information across services and devices in order to piece together the most complete profile of us they can. The more complete the info, the more valuable our profile is when companies sell it to third parties.

These dossiers being assembled on us are made still more valuable by corporate identity policing measures, like Facebook's awful "real names" (or "authentic names") policy. But it's not just about marketing. Such policies should be a serious cause for alarm in a culture where immigrants are being rounded up. When Donald

J. Trump talks about his idea for a "Muslim registry," some people (myself included) publicly remarked that Facebook has already done this work for him. And this is a terrible reality.

Few people have a clear idea about which systems can be trusted completely, which systems should never be trusted, and which systems need to watched very carefully. Worse, many online companies, including some of the big ones you'd think you could trust, have made it their business to take advantage of that confusion and misplaced trust. They leverage privacy laws that are way behind the times to collect, sell, and trade your private information as data, in their databases.

For example, if you send or communicate something private while at work, at school, or on Facebook, it might not actually be private. It might not even be "yours" anymore—legally and, to some degree, practically speaking. The places where you experience private time online and even on your phone are watched and monitored by the companies who host those services, too.

Companies like Twitter, Google, and Facebook need to convince you to share your private information because their advertisers "need" access to what rightfully belongs to you. Apps are the worst offenders, because they take more information about you than they need, and you get little choice in the matter if you want to use the app at all.

That's a problem because it takes away your control over information that could say more about you and even your physical location than you want anyone to know. Like your identifying information and metadata (detailed background information on you) that these companies collect when you use their services.

If all of this makes you feel overwhelmed, that's understandable—and it's okay. A big part of this book is about thwarting data collection and defying surveillance.. It's one of the ways you can practice resistance every day. In this book you'll learn where your info is leaking and what apps, devices, and social media sites are snitching on you. You also figure out which ways are best for you when it comes to defending yourself against, and pushing back on, surveillance.

You don't need to quit social media, or stop doing things you love online. You don't need to become a shadowy underground hacker. This book will help you individuate your experience with tech, privacy, and security so you can make the safest choices for you and the people you care about. And after reading even the first couple of chapters, you'll find it gets much easier to stop companies from spying on you, and to get everything under control.

Anonymity on mailing lists and social media

Everyone, of every gender and orientation, wants the option to be anonymous online. Anonymity is becoming synonymous with freedom. For many, it represents safety. And for some, like domestic violence victims, LGBT people, democracy activists, or people of color, it can mean the difference between life and death.

The problem is, the surveillance state we're in prevents many people from having anonymity. This is especially true online where we might want to be actively sharing and learning, but can't afford to expose our daily, personal lives. And our interests should be no one's business, unless we want to share. If we want to be on a mailing list on unions but don't want people on it Googling our work details, or have the whole world know we're interested in email discussions about sex worker's rights, that should be our decision, not someone else's.

Online anonymity is never perfect. Even the best hackers in the world screw up when it comes to anonymity nowadays. That's how we know—because they got caught. Yet there are still ways to protect your identity and keep prying eyes off your digital trail. What's important to know is that context is important. Wanting to keep yourself "anonymous" on an email list is going to be vastly different than anonymity on social media, and even that'll be different depending on what kind of device you're using.

Of course, to protect the people you send email to in a group, the "BCC" function is essential. It's also the number one thing people tend to screw up, exposing their email list to itself, allowing everyone on it to see… everyone on it. More and more people find this upsetting, yet it still happens. The way to avoid being one of the exposed people is to sign up to your lists with an email address that's separate from your everyday or work email.

There are many free options for getting a new address, and most services will let you route the email to your regular email address—this is called "forwarding" or making a "rule." Make sure it's a secure, encrypted service. Be sure to read the section in this book about using a VPN or Tor, so you know how to keep your IP address off the new email you're setting up. And be sure to diligently use the VPN (Or Tor) every time you use that address.

You'll want to make sure that the new email address isn't with a service that will combine your account with one you already have. So, if you have a Google account (Gmail, YouTube, or other service), then you'll want your secondary email address to be with a non-Google service. This way, you don't have to worry about Google trying to combine your personas, and you also don't have to worry about making a mistake and forgetting to log out and back in again. This is a common mistake.

With a fully separate address and a VPN, you'll have a strong separate email to use for mailing lists, signing up for social media accounts, or other uses. This setup is great for most everyone who wants to keep their "real name" off an email list.

Still, it won't be completely anonymous. There are too many factors out of your control to ensure full anonymity. For instance, you can't hide or change what's called a "MAC address" on your phone or tablet; that's the identifying number associated with the Wi-Fi chip in your device. You also can't completely control the tracking and background data collection going on through your browser. One answer is to use a completely separate device for your emailing, Tweeting, Facebooking, etc.—and I tell you how to use things like "burner" phones in Chapter 4, "Your phone is a tracking device." But that's yet another step to follow and remember, which you may not need or even want to bother with, because figuring out who is associated with a MAC address is for an advanced adversary.

Being truly anonymous is practically rocket science these days, but behaving anonymously online is a matter of knowing your way around privacy and security. What many people find better than anonymity is learning to keep separate profiles, and keeping identities firmly separated.

Identity, and keeping things separate

Many people prefer to keep their work, family, and social personas separate. In fact, for most people it's practically required if they want to maintain a professional reputation, or simply keep their jobs. Separation of identities (also called "compartmentalization") is also crucial for keeping family members like children safe online. For people who are likely to be targeted for violence, like domestic abuse survivors or those who do politically dangerous work, separated identities online can be the difference between life and death.

It's not that you're doing anything wrong; this is simply how many societies function. Only recently have we been led to believe that people who have different identities are somehow doing something bad. That's thanks to social media sites like Facebook who force "real names" policies on users (because it's lucrative for selling advertising data sets), with the false claim that people won't behave badly without anonymity.

You probably already keep your work life and your private life separated. If you're going to become more active, whether a little bit online or a lot in public protests, you'll need to assess how much compartmentalization is best for you.

In Chapter 3, "Hack-proof your life," you'll do a social media cleanup. This helps you see how your privacy settings show you to the world and people you're connected to, and you get a handle on how much separation (or not) is between your different areas of life, like school, work, family, and friends. In the next section I'll tell you how to find and remove as much personal information as possible from the Internet, specifically with "people search" websites.

But you've probably noticed just how hard social media and apps make it when you want to have different lives or personas. Websites you sign into and apps you install or make new accounts with will often cross-match you in the background. You can tell because they'll auto-fill information you didn't give them, or grab an icon photo of yours from another site. Facebook, for example, has a nasty habit of "recommending" people to be your friend after rifling through your address book. The same is happening to other people who have, or obtain, your phone number or email address. Facebook has even, in the past, recommended strangers "friend" each other by using each person's phone location data.

Some sites will let you create multiple accounts. But they're never really separate or secret unless you do some really inconvenient things to appear as a fully separate person. It's not impossible, though the more separate you want one identity to be, the trickier it gets. And the more vigilant you need to be in order to keep nosy companies and authorities out of your personal business.

There is a lot to know about identity separation, and it is detailed throughout this book. The basics are:

- When creating a new account, use a different email address, phone number, or anything else required for sign-up.
- Use a separate phone if you are doing communications or posting media.
- Before you connect to the internet with your separate identity (or create a new account), make sure you've installed and turned on a recommended VPN (Virtual Private Network), or Tor ("The Onion Router").

- Don't friend yourself or anyone you know.
- If you're not using a VPN, Tor, or Tails use a separate browser.
- Use encrypted chat apps.
- Don't click on URLs sent via direct message from people you don't know; this can capture your IP address or hack your device.
- Pictures can leak all kinds of information about you, even your location; remove its metadata ("EXIF" data) before sharing.
- Don't get hacked.
- Don't do or say anything that could contaminate your separate identity.

If an account gets "contaminated," you'll need to stop using it. For instance, if you're using something to obscure your IP address when you sign in on one account, like Tor, Tails or a VPN, you must do that every single time. Read more about VPNs, Tor and the Tails operating system in Chapter 5, "Defy Surveillance." The one time you forget, it's over; the account will now have the wrong (that is, your real) IP address stored in the account's records on the company's home server.

Keep in mind that there are a lot of ways to identify you, even if your IP address is 'randomized' with Tor. Be sure to delete your browser cache, history and cookies—some browsers allow "anonymous sessions." Do not log into existing accounts that contain your personally identifying information (unless you're sure that's what you want to do). Stick to sites that use "https" so your traffic has end-to-end encryption. Visit the Tor Project's website (torproject.org) for even more information on how to safely use Tor.

Some apps want you to link your Facebook, Twitter, Flickr, Instagram, and other accounts with them. The problem is, if all of those accounts are linked, someone needs to crack only that one app to have access to all of those accounts. The other problem is that if you're trying to keep your online identities separate, linking sign-ins or services will contaminate your separate accounts. So will using multiple Google accounts; the company likes to link identities. If you do choose to link any accounts, make sure each is an information dead-end for malicious attackers or spying.

Keeping identities separate can be a careful and precise routine, or a lot of work--usually both. Decide who you're keeping these identities separate from so you can decide how far to take it. Is it from the public? Is it from anyone who can see records on a website you visit? Is it from someone who is spying on your network traffic/Internet connections? Is it from someone who might examine your computer with forensic tools? I highly recommend that no matter what your answers are here that you read the post "Domain Games: Role-playing an online identity" (exposingtheinvisible.org/resources/watching-out-yourself/domain-games/).

Like all aspects of security, identity separation is a rabbit hole that can go deep into Internet conspiracy land, as well as offer dangerously bad advice. Check the "Resources" chapter for solid recommendations on taking your compartmentalization research further.

Focus your fight
What made you want to spring into action? It might've been one

thing that made you realize you couldn't just sit still and watch the news go by. A photo, a video, a story about something that made you say, "no more." Or it might be an accumulation of feelings over time, a gradual (or incrementally fast) build up until you realized that something was really wrong. Maybe a collection of stories, or finding out that one really bad thing happened, and as much as you hoped otherwise, the balance of power was wrong and justice would not be happening. It could be someone you know being hurt, or someone enough like you to make you realize that it's only a matter of time until … it might be too late to do something to stop it.

One of the signs we've seen repeated at protests around the US in the beginning of 2017 has read, "First they came for the Muslims… and we said not today." This was in reaction to Donald Trump's executive actions on immigration, keeping in line with his words and policies to ban people based on their religion (and also, obviously their skin color). These signs accompanied others with sayings like "No ban, no wall" and "Immigrants make America great," scrawled on pizza and Amazon boxes—then shown and shared on Snapchat, Instagram, Twitter, and more.

The "First they came" saying comes from a poem written by Martin Niemöller in the years following World War II, after he survived two concentration camps. The poem is about apathy, and at the same time it's about collective action and civil rights. It's about how something like the Holocaust happens when we do nothing in the face of corrupt power, and when we don't speak out when bad things happen to other people. Above all, it's about empathy, and not just letting things happen. It goes like this:

"First they came for the Socialists, and I did not speak out—
Because I was not a Socialist.

Then they came for the Trade Unionists, and I did not speak out—

Because I was not a Trade Unionist.

Then they came for the Jews, and I did not speak out—

Because I was not a Jew.

Then they came for me—and there was no one left to speak for me."

The piece is a dire warning about the costs of complacency. Angela Davis gave it a visceral edge when she wrote, "If they come for me in the morning, they will come for you in the night."

It's as relevant today as ever while we fight Facebook's censorship creep and fake news culture, and as we become determined to stay awake and resist any "new normal" seeping from the White House.

As it is inspiring, the piece reminds us that there are many battles to fight. It's easy to feel worn down by the daily onslaught of bad and crazy news. It's also easy to feel rage fatigue, and overwhelm at the amount of issues at hand.

Chapter 2, "Self-Care Rules Everything Around Me (SCREAM)" gives you tools and guidance with the rage, the overwhelm, the trolls and haters, and even the down times. But you have to get started by focusing your fight. If you decide to join five different organizations on five different issues, you'll simply spread yourself too thin.

Many people feel pulled to one issue, and that's perfect. But some people see a lot of different fires, and feel like they need to attend to all of them—except that's how you lose your social media audience, get stressed or depressed, and end up giving less to everything.

If that's you, think about the issues that give you the strongest feelings of urgency. Write them down. Then prioritize them, and narrow the list down. Pick two or three (at the most) to make your main focus. Don't worry about the other issues yet. Just because you make Planned Parenthood, immigration reform, democratic voting or Black Lives Matter your main focus, it doesn't mean you're not going to jump into action when police injustice happens locally, or when we all need to go to the airports again.

Seven ways to resist every day
One of the affectionate nicknames given to this book by hackers who helped me with research is "The Resistance Cookbook." And maybe this book is one part subversive, two parts "chicken soup for the resistance."

That word—"resist"—means different things to different people.

Resisting is what we do when we question what we're being presented with: Something unjust, hurtful, or abuse portrayed as "normal," necessary, or harmless. To resist means to push back against oppression and to allow yourself to get angry and passionate in the face of racism, sexism, abuse, and any way in which populations are harmed, devalued, or made powerless. When we resist, we do so because we seek a just and fair world, and are willing to do something about it.

Resistance takes many forms. It can be marching in the streets, it can be sharing something on social media, or it can be telling your friend who stood up to an online bully that you're proud of them. It could entail putting together a website for organizing information or protests, or it might be bringing snacks and drinks to the people working all night on it. Resisting might mean making videos where you interview people affected by injustice, or writing an article on your experience at a protest.

Here are seven ways you can resist right now, and every day:

- Install an encrypted chat app like Signal or WhatsApp on your phone, and get one friend to do it, too.
- Find an article or video that sheds light on an injustice and share it on social media.
- Review your privacy settings with Google, Facebook, Twitter, Instagram, Flickr and any other sites you use, and limit all the data collecting you can.
- When you see a wrongful abuse of power, like President Trump using family members in his cabinet, remind your social media followers that this is not normal, or okay.
- Make a donation to the ACLU, The National Lawyers Guild, Planned Parenthood, EFF, or any organization that is in line with your values.
- Sign an online petition. Even if it feels like it won't affect change, people see it–and, especially, so do press and media.
- Tell a friend or family member who went to a protest that you're proud of them.

That last bullet point is about one of the hardest parts of resisting:

how it feels. Being a digital revolutionary means you're often the first one to do something. The first one in your family, the first one in your social circle, the first one in your relationship, or even the first one... ever.

Sometimes it also means you're the first one to speak up about a lie, a problem, a sexist or racist act, hypocrisy, or something that just doesn't add up. You may be the first one to use technology in a certain way. Or the first one to point out a problem, a flaw, a way it can be broken or misused. The consequences for being the first person can be awful. Or elevating. But usually, it's hard. Speaking up comes with support and attacks, not always in equal measure. It's harder when people who you want to see listen to you, don't.

Being a revolutionary is about taking what you've learned here and putting your own spin on it. Your appetite for doing things in innovative ways is real, despite the initiative, resolve and risk-taking involved. As a result, your own independent movement only results in growth.

You're most likely straddling your passion for change with a full time job, school, or your family (or all three). Some of you will take the leap to make your passion full time, or to make some sacrifices with time and money to work toward change. Most people have to balance being part of the resistance with the rest of their lives, and to do that they focus their time and attention to specific areas of resisting. You can embody values of the resistance with balance, and yes, you can protest capitalism even if you have to work at McDonald's.

Joining the resistance starts with passion for a cause; fighting against injustice, for equal rights, to save the planet, for healthcare, to disrupt corruption and hypocrisy among those in power, to smash sexism or racism, and to keep progress from sliding backward. This passion is what gets you willing to speak out, share ideas, get out the door for a protest or march; make and share photos, videos, artwork, and writing; go out to a meeting for organizing campaigns, or to volunteer where it matters most. But the most effective agents of change know that this is a marathon, and not a short race.

Some people might try to tell you that by taking a stand or speaking out against injustices, you're somehow "asking for it." Don't fall for this. Just because a woman wears a skirt, is she "asking for" sexual assault? Of course not. There's no doubt that attracting attention to yourself about controversial issues is going to make you a target. Trolling and attacks are meant to silence us, so we won't stand up for ourselves or those who need support.

You'll find help, strength, tools for success, and sustenance in this book. Being a revolutionary, and resisting, is about resilience.

This book is where resistance and resilience become part of your DNA.

CHAPTER 2
SELF-CARE RULES EVERYTHING AROUND ME (SCREAM)

Deportations. The threat of war. Fear of losing health insurance. Brazen hate crimes. Climate science disavowed. LGBT rights in jeopardy. Life's stresses are enough, but now all this, too? If you feel overwhelmed, you're far from alone. Everyone is trying to figure out how to cope with the chaos, the outrage, and the endless stream of bad news.

In a 2016 survey, Pew Internet Research Center found that "more than one-third of social media users are worn out by the amount of political content they encounter, and more than half describe their online interactions with those they disagree with politically as stressful and frustrating." And it feels like the disturbing news sometimes comes in faster than we can parse it.

It's become commonplace that we wake up and something totally unexpected and crazy has happened. Like a white supremacist being handed a role typically reserved for generals, or the disavowal of climate science by the new federal government. Five minutes later, we find out our country has bombed another country without warning or proper governmental approval. It's like we're in a world-politics horror film and we're all the "final girl."

We have to stay awake and informed, and keep up the resistance. Giving up or becoming complacent would be like giving a gift to those abusing power. It's more urgent than ever that we don't disassociate from what's happening to our communities and our government. Yet being well informed feels like a constant challenge to our energy reserves—to put it mildly. We are in danger of outrage fatigue.

Staying sane

It's a lot easier to resist—to organize, work toward change, fight fake news, support allies, and share reality-check information—when we feel hopeful and strong enough to fight. But a lot of people spent the first few months after America's 2016 election feeling scared and depressed, frantically checking their phones every five minutes for the next batch of I-can't-believe-it's-happening news. We can't—and shouldn't—check out on what's happening in Washington, the UN, or elsewhere. Staying informed is critical, especially for those of us who feel a responsibility to do something. Yet we also have to stay sane, which means balancing our media consumption, activism, emotions, and mental health.

It's best to focus on one thing you want to change; it will be overwhelming to think you need to change everything. Remember to just spend time with people not focused on resistance, too.

Take periods of rest. One psychologist consulted for this book explained that it's common for people to feel they're not doing enough when they're marching and doing protests every weekend. Nobody can keep up that schedule.

Do an assessment of your news sources; trim your feeds and notifications. You only need one or two breaking news sources. Cut out media sources that scream the worst-case scenarios from their headlines, and ones that seem like they want you to run from the room screaming about nuclear war.

Rather than getting a tweet from Reuters every ten minutes, consider following individual people (like reporters, organizations, or activists whose interests are the same as yours) that share news as it happens. Follow people who help you stay awake, and let people you trust curate your news a bit.

Drinking from the firehose will kill you.

Create time to read the news and process your panic. I read the news when I wake up, over coffee, for about an hour. Then I make myself get up and do something else—exercise, work, chores, a meeting, etc. I might go back to reading the news afterward, but that one sanity break per day works wonders. It also makes me react better later, when I read more news.

Establish a baseline

Figure out a baseline of hours each day for you to spend on news reading and social media. Then make a determined plan on how many hours are reasonable. This is your target.

While you don't need to be hard on yourself about hitting that exact target, it'll give you something to assess your behavior with and mitigate the damage of overwhelm. For instance, one psychologist consulted for this book told me, "I know that I personally was spending nearly four hours a day on news, and finally had to decide an hour was enough."

Remove news outlets that make your feeds repetitive, and ones that are more sensationalism than informed reporting. If you feel like you need to keep an eye on the hysterical sources, move them to a secondary list so they're not in your face.

Many people are feeling the bad news overload and are creating solutions that put all the resist-related news in digest form. A digest cuts way back on the overwhelm by putting your information consumption of worrying news in one place, that you read when you're feeling ready to get caught up. It omits the feeling of being barraged, and the impulse to constantly check for developments. One great site doing this is whatthefuckjusthappenedtoday.com. Many groups and news sites also do email digest newsletters you can subscribe to, and even sites like old Digg are putting all its daily Trump news into one post.

Next, do an inventory of your notifications. You don't need to get a notification for everything, or from everyone. Seriously: Go look at your notifications settings right now and make some choices.

Make reasonable weekly goals—or rules—for the number of emails you send, calls you make to representatives, or minimum donations to organizations. For the time being, there will be a new urgent issue every damn week, and you need to spend your energy smartly.

Automation: keep it going when you need a break

You may not realize it, but much of what you're doing can be tasked to robots. That is, robots in the form of automation tools that can do everything from auto-posting to different social media sites for you, to organizing your reading for later.

Automated tools will vary by their functions and limitations, and even by country. In the U.S., we have a few apps and bots that can do some of the heavy lifting for us—things like calling and faxing government officials to hold them accountable. More appear to be on their way. Not everyone will have access to such tools—they may not be available in your country, for example–but that's likely to change as new software packages are developed.

If you maintain a social media presence, auto-posting is a sanity saver when you need to make sure all your accounts get updated. It's also potentially important when time is of the essence. Being ready to auto-update your social media will be great when you want to use one app to document an event while automatically having your posts and media also uploaded to Facebook, Flickr, or other sites. IFTTT.com (If This Then That) is a very flexible site where you can use a variety of "recipes" to fill your auto-posting needs. Some tools, like Tweetdeck, will post for you on a schedule. This allows you to plan announcements and re-posts—or take a break without disappearing from the world.

Use a bookmarking tool or RSS reader. Some good ones are Instapaper, Pocket, Feedly, Pinterest, Evernote, or Flipboard. Consolidate your news consumption and information collecting by automating how you read it and save it for later. For instance with the free service Instapaper, you can create folders for each topic you're interested in. When you see an article you want to read, add it to the Instapaper folder according to its subject with one click, where it will be saved. Then read your articles when you make time, instead of every five minutes.

Automation tools to save your sanity:

* Save news for later with an RSS reader or bookmarking tool

- Auto-post with IFTTT (If This Then That)
- Schedule tweets and posts
- Set up AmazonSmile, ResistBot, Five Calls, Daily Action
- Use a monitoring tool from SocDir

Consider automating small donations to organizations you want to support; even $1 a month is helpful, and if it can come out of your credit card or bank account without any effort and minimal impact, then you're done. A significant number of people use Amazon Smile to choose small ways to donate as they shop. When customers shop on AmazonSmile (smile.amazon.com), the AmazonSmile Foundation donates 0.5% of the price of eligible purchases to an organization of your choosing. If your priority topic has an associated nonprofit, it's probably on Amazon's list. There are over one million eligible 501(c)(3) public charitable organizations available to donate to via Amazon.

In the U.S., automate calling your representatives and your call schedule with a service like Five Calls. Use Resistbot to turn text messages into faxes and send them to your elected officials for you. Just text "resist" to 50409; then Resistbot asks for your name and zip code to determine who your elected officials are, and asks you to write what you want to say.

With Daily Action (dailyaction.org) you enter your zip code and get one daily action texted to you; this way you can just focus on that and feel you've done something.

Groups to join
Join a group, online or offline, or both. Groups have a lot of

shortcuts and sanity-savers already figured out. Plus, if you're new to resisting, organizing, politics or activism, you're better off not starting a whole new group on your own. Save your energy, and make an already existing group stronger with it.

Finding community in the face of oppression is one of the ultimate acts of resistance. Without community in a time of fear and stress, we can feel distanced, depressed, disconnected, or even ill. With a group, your voice and ability to affect change is multiplied. Communities provide information and tools. They'll also keep your stress levels in check. Your shared experience for a cause or shared interest means that you have skills to share, and there will people dealing with the same problems you are.

As with many automation tools, finding groups is something specific to your country or region. Generally, you might need to do some sleuthing and searching to find your group; social media searches and Googling for news articles about activism in your area is your first stop for finding community outside the U.S.

In the wake of the 2016 election here in America, hundreds of grassroots groups formed to oppose the new White House regime. Some came from experienced political operatives; others were launched by people who were brand new to activism. A significant number of groups were formed during bus, car, and plane trips to the Women's March. Some will be a better fit for you than others, so don't worry about doing a little shopping or having to change groups if yours isn't working for you. Being in a group can feel like a struggle sometimes, but remember: In our digital revolutionary times, it only takes one significant act to change the landscape.

The most recommended resource for finding a group in the U.S.

is Indivisible Guide (indivisibleguide.com). It was started when current and former congressional staffers created a guide on Google Docs outlining how regular people could effectively connect with their representatives, and have their messages heard. It was built on the Tea Party's model of locally-focused organizing and aggressive strategies—thankfully without the Tea Party's tactics of name-calling and spitting on those who oppose their views. Indivisible's website has you enter your zip code to find like-minded communities and groups.

The "matchmaking" approach that Indivisible uses with zip codes is taken a step further with Movement Match. This site features a quiz that matches you with the right organization.

My favorite matchmaking site isn't going to be featured uncensored on prime time anytime soon. Holy Fuck The Election (holyfucktheelection.com) is a cheeky, foul-mouthed, and useful site for finding organizations that need help. Visit the page and it starts by asking "What's on your mind?" You're presented with a set of choices to click on, like "Electing some fucking Democrats" and "Not getting grabbed by the fucking pussy." The site then asks which you can spare: Money or time? Then you're served up organizations that match your interests and commitment level.

Find your group:

- Indivisible Guide (indivisibleguide.com)
- Movement Match (jointhemovementtoday.weebly.com)
- Holy Fuck The Election (holyfucktheelection.com)
- Town Hall Project (townhallproject-86312.firebaseapp.com)

- 350 (350.org)
- flippable (flippable.org)

There are oodles of groups to choose from, and far too many to list here. Here are some to get you inspired and thinking about where you'd like to plug in: There's The Women's March on Washington, #ResistTrumpTuesdays (from The Working Families Party, MoveOn, and People's Action); the ACLU, Planned Parenthood , Internet Defense League, and the EFF. Also consider Black Lives Matter, the Black Youth Project 100, the Dream Defenders and the Million Hoodies Movement for Justice.

Sleeping Giants focuses on activism through getting online ads pulled. There's also United Resistance (which includes the Center for Biological Diversity, United We Dream, and the Ella Baker Center for Human Rights). In addition, check out Lambda Legal, Equality New York, GLAAD, Gays Against Guns, Coming Out Muslim and the Trans Latina Network.

Trust but verify: Poison people
Unfortunately, groups and activism can attract toxic people. You know, the person who manipulates, uses people, has massive empathy problems, and avoids accountability for their actions at every turn—sometimes dramatically. They're inconsistent, have honesty issues, claim "victim" status when they want to get their way, and will use upsetting information as a means of control. This person probably also likes to make people prove themselves to them, takes credit for the work of others, and keeps everyone on the defensive. They traffic in trust, but flip out when you try to verify why

they should be trusted. This person splinters groups, turns people against each other, and hold back progress. They're sometimes suspected of being sent by the opposition to ruin the group on purpose, but more often than not they're just … toxic.

The poison person is especially problematic in communities that champion secret-keeping (privacy), confidentiality or anonymity; advocate for vulnerable or at-risk populations; or deal with information known by few. In these groups, toxic people can gain total control over a situation based on the fear people already have about being outed, and hold information hostage. The narcissistic toxic person splits people into camps, and isolates people to get more control. This kind of person will also share "deep" secrets with you, while being gossipy or judgmental about others.

Poisoning of groups by a toxic person has happened more than once in hacker communities over the last decade. These destructive people seem to thrive on communities that need to keep secrets. The incidents with these groups were coupled with sexual abuse, worsened by the fact that some were same-sex encounters with people who were terrified of being outed. But because hacker communities never know if what they're doing is legal or not, people were afraid of retribution for trying to stop both the splintering of the group, and the abuse.

They were also protected by people who either truly didn't get abuse of power dynamics, or hoped to avoid disrupting the status quo. When people tried to report and seek help with the toxic person, the victims were shocked (and essentially sentenced to more abuse) when leadership in their anti-authoritarian groups asked why they didn't go to the police. The toxic people in these cases serially ruined great groups, as well as served to harm the kinds of people those groups were supposed to be fighting for.

The people I just described seem to take pleasure in what they do, but not all toxic people are aware of what they're doing. Either way, they create stress and complexity where it's unneeded. Poison people are draining, too. They leave you feeling wiped out, and in groups they seem to absorb all the group's attention and energy.

However, unless you're a licensed psychotherapist, and happen to be the poison person's actual therapist, you can't diagnose, treat, or fix this person. You're simply not qualified for it. At the same time, it's pointless to hurt or traumatize someone by expulsion or accusations if they're unaware of their behavior. There are things you can do to protect yourself and your group, and course-correct before it's too late:

Trust, but verify. Toxic people get away with a lot because they take advantage of people's trust. Give them the same benefit of the doubt as you would anyone else, but verify their claims. Especially if they say that what they're doing or saying is okay with someone who isn't present to consent or agree. Someone with nothing to hide shouldn't have a problem with this.

Set limits. Boundaries are critical with these energy vampires. Be polite but firm about saying no, or stating that you're done with a conversation because it's not productive. You don't need to agree, consent, or go along with anything just to be polite. A non-poison person will respect your boundaries.

Don't get sucked in. Stay in control of your emotions at all times around the toxic person. They will trigger your emotions, woo you with false kindness, or put you on the defensive to manipulate and take advantage of you. Stay calm, cool, and collected around the troublemaker and don't get pulled into their drama. They may try to needle you, but if you don't react the way they want, they'll move on to people who will. If no one falls for their drama traps, they'll leave altogether.

Stay focused on solutions. Being solutions-oriented is practically the opposite of being a toxic person. They never are, unless the solution puts them in the spotlight or gives them leverage—and it's usually a bad solution. Poison people make conversations and groups stray away from finding a solution to any problem at hand. Derail their drama or manipulation by saying, "How can we fix this?" Or, "What should be done so we can move forward?" Another one is, "How can we make sure this doesn't happen again?" Stay on target to find a solution.

Demand straight answers. Poison people avoid accountability at all costs, and will go to extremes to avoid a satisfactory answer. Ask them "why" a lot, and make good use of yes or no questions. Restate your questions when they try to derail you, and don't give up. If they claim to be acting on someone else's behalf, insist on including that person in your conversation.

Don't forget wrongdoing. If they apologize, thank them—if it's a real "I'm sorry" and not an excuse presented as an apology. But don't forget what they've done, or you won't be cautious against a repeat offense.

Don't indulge a narcissist. They'll seek constant approval, gossip and judge, make you feel sorry for them, and tell you something awful (unprompted) while demanding secrecy. These are the warning signs of someone pulling your strings. Do an assessment of the people close to you; make boundaries and set limits with anyone who is constantly taking from you (emotionally) and never giving anything back. For instance, if you walk away from a conversation feeling like you just gave a ton of support and they didn't even ask how you're doing (or did so as an afterthought), back off from that relationship.

Always have witnesses. The poisonous group member divides people into camps, pits people against one another, and always isolates their victims. Keep your contact with the toxic person in public or group settings—they hate nothing more than witnesses to their behavior. They'll be able to pull less and less drama the more people see what's going on, especially if the problem person creates problems but avoids or refuses to solve them. Never confront or engage meaningfully with the toxic person unless you have allies or witnesses around.

Toxic people like to have an easy time poisoning the pot and playing out their narcissistic dramas. If they don't get what they want from one person, they'll keep trying others; if no one gets sucked in and they keep getting held accountable, they'll flame out and leave on their own. When things work out, the problem individual causes so many problems without solutions that they get themselves ejected by leadership.

Your group will need to repair itself. Holistic Security (holistic-security.tacticaltech.org) has fantastic guides and resources to help groups manage stress and fear, and great suggestions for managing interpersonal group conflict.

Surveillance, bad news, trolls: Feeling overwhelmed

Injustice is an attack: We feel like we're being attacked. Power abuse is a violation: We feel violated. Knowing we're being tracked and surveilled by companies and authorities makes us feel helpless and angry. Where there is abuse of power, sexism, racism, xenophobia, or other attacks on someone's right to exist or choose, there are trolls and haters. Nothing gets the psychos lathered up like speaking truth to power, especially if you've caught them doing something wrong or pushing false information.

The news cycle—just waking up and reading the news every day—is the hardest part for many people. Sometimes it feels like the bad news won't stop, and it traps us in negative emotions like anger, stress or depression. Sometimes, it will feel like it'll last forever.

Think of it like a storm: These things blow in, rage for a while, but they'll eventually go back out to sea. That's not to say there might be another storm coming in later, or feel like it'll never stop raining, but these things will eventually change. Plus, there are ways to cope.

What's going on inside? The answer is: A perfectly reasonable, but unpleasant response. If you're under attack, you're probably feeling:

- Anxiety, fear, and/or anger
- Detachment, like you're an outsider to your own life
- Unsafe, even when it makes no sense to feel this way
- Guilt, shame, and self-blame
- Mistrust and betrayal
- Depression and hopelessness
- Alienation and loneliness

- Embarrassment and exposure

When things hit you really hard you might experience:

- Intrusive, upsetting thoughts or memories that can come on suddenly
- Unreliable memory, such as difficulty remembering exact details
- Nightmares and insomnia
- Irritability, easily annoyed
- Physical reactions such as a pounding heart, rapid breathing, nausea, muscle tension, or sweating
- Difficulty concentrating
- Avoidance of people, events, or situations

You may only feel some of the things mentioned here, or you may feel all of them. Many people who go through periods of online attack find they cycle through these feelings, sometimes repeatedly. The cycling can vary in intensity, until one day it's just less powerful. It's okay to feel and experience all of these things. This sucks, but it's normal.

When you're under attack, make sure you show these lists to people who care about you so they know what you're going through. Reading the list will give them an idea of what's going on if you have anxiety, get depressed, snap at them out of the blue, or can't sleep. It'll also help people understand so they can give you the support and room you need to conquer this madness.

Self-care guidelines

You may have noticed that most of these feelings look a lot like grief. In fact, grief may be the response you're processing to whatever made you realize that something needed to be done to change the world we're in. Many people reported feeling grief after the 2016 election in the US, and it's not a coincidence.

But like grief, online attacks and worldview trauma can feel like it goes away, but can sometimes come rushing back. Like just when you feel like you're doing okay, one trigger will bring back that feeling in your chest or your stomach, and the emotional spiral begins again. You might feel like it will never end, but it will. The annoying part is that there won't be one single moment when the way you feel inside just ends. But one day, you'll realize that you haven't felt upset in a long time, and that's when you'll know you're through it.

Until then, here are some ways to deal with those feelings. I'm an advisor for Without My Consent (withoutmyconsent.org), a resource of legal options for stalking, revenge porn, and online harassment. Our website describes steps you can take on the road to emotional recovery, which begin with taking active, practical steps to address the problem.

Talk to an attorney or law enforcement if someone has threatened you, including "doxing" you—publishing your private information online. A formal complaint process might feel more stressful, especially if you're campaigning against police brutality or injustices in the criminal justice system. But this kind of active coping with the situation helps some people feel better more quickly, and may strengthen your resolve to push the system into positive change. It will also deflect those who defend abusers by accusing their targets of inaction.

As I mentioned in the previous section, addressing your feelings is important. So is not going through any of this alone, even the daily overwhelm of bad news. Talk to people who care about you regularly, and don't be reluctant to chat with a counselor or therapist. You'd be surprised how helpful it can be to talk to someone who doesn't know you, and who you don't need to "trade" support with.

Talking to people who support your political fight will make you feel less alone, let you swap stories about dealing with all this, and you'll feel safer. Writing it out helps, too—a blog is good for getting your stress and anger out, and you don't need to publish it or make it public. It can be a great way for writing out your reactions and arguments to attackers and opposition, for either release or practice.

Doing something every day—especially little things—that make you feel good (like exercising, experiencing natural beauty, massage) is important. So is finding a way to relax and de-stress. That can include listening to music, watching a favorite show, playing video games, reading a non-political book, or meditation. Many people find religious or spiritual practices help a lot, too. A glass of wine is great for unwinding, but try not to depend or go overboard on drugs or booze, because these substances can make things feel worse.

If the way you feel just won't give you a break and gets in the way of your relationships, jeopardizes your job or schoolwork, or keeps you from functioning normally (especially if you feel like you just can't take it any longer), reach out to someone who will help you weather the storms until they pass.

Find someone to talk to that has experience working with overwhelm, trauma, harassment, or abuse. What's most important is that you find someone you feel safe enough with to talk about what's going on and what you're going through. Some therapists will even see you online. If you want psychological support, consult the links and phone numbers in the "Resources" chapter at the end of this book.

Online attacks and trolls

Trolls and haters come with the territory of speaking up about injustice. Some people will try to make you feel like online attacks, trauma, and abuse are less real than "in-person" harassment. They may imply or tell you outright that it's somehow your fault that you got harassed. This blame game is used ubiquitously against women, people of color, and LGBT people. These qualifiers alone will target you for attack. But the blame game is commonly employed against anyone who speaks up online for a cause, so you're a likely target whenever you speak out against discrimination, abuse, racism, sexism, or hypocrisy. Online harassers will also try to dismiss you what you say by devaluing you as a person. They'll claim you have a grudge, or that you're being "too sensitive."

Remind yourself not to waste your energy on such attacks. Follow the guidelines in this chapter for dealing with poison people. Stay calm, cool, collected and graceful as much as possible. At least 99.9% of the time, people who spend their time attacking you online are not worth your time and attention in response.

If you feel there is a real reason to respond to an attacker, insist on being solutions-oriented. Are they really trying to fix something, or are they just trying to derail you? Can they provide a legitimate citation for any factual claims they make? Do they really care about the topic, or do they just care about saying you're wrong? Like with poison people, asking your attacker "why" to most of their statements is enough to reveal they're full of it, and just out to hurt people and cause drama.

Don't forget that being attacked online is no joke. When someone attacks you online, it's real. It's abuse and harassment. Despite what some social media sites may cling to as a defense, and authorities still refuse to acknowledge, these things are as real and harmful online as they are off. The only difference is a punch.

Online harassment increases your vulnerability to sexual violence, can cause real emotional harm, and can ruin your reputation. It communicates to the world that it's okay to devalue us and invites others to participate in harassing, humiliating, and hurting us. But none of us deserves to lose our jobs, our friends, custody of our kids, our personal safety, our emotional well-being, or our sanity just for standing up for our values.

When the haters and trolls attack, remember to stay calm, online and off. Don't be hard on yourself, and take steps to strengthen your mental and emotional health in real life. Eat, sleep, and get support from friends who care about you, from people fighting for the same issues you are, or even a counselor or therapist. When you look for someone to talk to outside your circles, evaluate them to make sure they're the right fit in terms of understanding your need to uses tech and stay connected. Find a list of therapists who "get" tech issues at smartprivacy.tumblr.com/therapists.

It's okay to change your account settings to private for a while if you need some time off, or to create a cushion of time during which the haters will find someone else to go bother. Some sites (such as Twitter) have simple on/off-style privacy settings, and others (like Facebook) have more-nuanced options for limiting access to your profile. Block and mute anyone, anytime, and you'll feel much better for doing so. Whatever you do, don't let the trolls beat you. Keep your social media accounts open; don't "quit the Internet."

When you're being serially abused, harassed, or stalked, file a police report to put the harassment on the record—but don't expect the police to do anything. Having a record of the abuse is better than not, though, and you can use the report number to get your personal information de-listed from data broker powerhouses like Lexis-Nexus and Intelius. Talk to a lawyer if you want to explore the possibility of pursuing legal action. Find a directory at withoutmyconsent.org.

If your attacker posts false, harmful, personal or offensive information or images about you, report them immediately to the website or social network. Read about how you can fight "doxing" (when attackers post personal information about you online) in the next chapter.

Start a file with details about your report. Make detailed records of everything you find. Take screencaps; for each image, note the date and time of posting and the screen name of the person that posted it. Download all the photos you find (they have hidden data on them); and save everything in a folder. There is a complete step-by-step process, advice, and templates for getting harmful things taken down (and repairing your reputation) in my book, *The Smart Girl's Guide to Privacy*.

Also consult Feminist Frequency's "Speak Up & Stay Safe(r)" guide (onlinesafety.feministfrequency.com) when combating attacks and harassment. It's for "anyone who fears they might be targeted, or who is already under attack, for speaking their mind online, but is especially designed for women, people of color, trans and genderqueer people, and everyone else whose existing oppressions are made worse by digital violence." It's not a highly technical guide, yet it's extremely thorough. It's indispensable if you need to be directly walked through a crisis.

CHAPTER 3

HACK-PROOF YOUR LIFE

The first order of business, no matter where you're at with any revolutions, digital or otherwise, is to take your privacy and security back into your own hands. But right now, the world of security isn't in our favor. Companies and even our own government is reckless and careless with our data: Breaches and theft are rampant. Attackers publish our private information online to silence us. No one tells us when our security has been compromised, and few companies bother to tell us how to protect ourselves when using their services.

Worse, we're under constant surveillance from authorities and greedy companies. Meanwhile, information security itself isn't exactly working on its outreach program. Hackers and infosec people, who are supposed to be working to protect us, tend to be the snootiest, least approachable people in the room. Many of us are afraid to even deal with them, let alone asking for non-technical explanations of anything.

Our security is critical for the revolution, because one of the big things we can all agree we're fighting for is to get our damn privacy back. And at the very least to tip the scales of imbalance back, because the people whose identities and privacy least protected by corporations like Facebook seem to be the people who are most at risk. Funny how that is.

Hack yourself

This chapter is where we get serious about thinking like a hacker. You're taking back your power over technology and communications, and you're using it to create change. It's the heart and soul of a digital revolution; it really is "power to the people." Thinking like a hacker here is the intersection of pushing back against the limitations we're presented with, and remaking those limitations to find empowerment. This is the heart of hacking, too. Hackers look for ways to "break" things to make them better, or to have a little fun.

Thinking like a hacker also means looking at something from the perspective of someone finding ways things can go wrong, or can be broken or misused. Hackers look for weaknesses to exploit, so to think like a hacker you need to look at your own online life to see what's vulnerable. Examine the social media sites, apps, and online services you use to find out where they expose your information and make you susceptible to attack or exploitation. I'm asking you to think like a creep as an act of self-protection—because the apps, sites, and services sure aren't protecting you.

At first, thinking like a hacker is a little intimidating. That's because cybersecurity is complicated and most of us feel helpless to protect ourselves. As if it's beyond our technical capabilities, and out of our power. But that's not the reality anymore. Things have changed: You have more power than you know, and there are way more "fighting back" tools available now than there were just five years ago.

Information security people and hackers have had their own awakening in that short amount of time, too. Many of them have decided to fight the imbalanced systems and make these tools for non-technical people like us to use. Encrypted apps like Signal and Disconnect, and the "Delete Me" service by Abine are perfect examples of what's happening in the "security by the people, for the people" revolution.

And this is exactly what this chapter is about. Staking your boundaries and taking your security and privacy back, and by using some of these revolutionary, cutting-edge tools. Once you get your security locked down, your privacy is protected and you only have to stick to your new security routines. Contrary to the way companies and authorities might make us feel, privacy is your right.

It should be up to you to decide what you want to keep private, not greedy companies or government wonks with a "collect it all" mentality about surveillance. Just as your ideals are worth doing something about, your privacy is worth protecting. As a resister, your personal life isn't supposed to be up for debate or attack. The social issues at hand are. Yet that's not how trolls and power-abusing authorities will see it. Which is why hardening your digital privacy and security is the best thing you can do for your mission, your well-being, and those around you—the people you care about.

Don't fret, cleaning up your private info online is a chore, but it comes with the reward of security. If you have a couple of close friends or family to do this with, team up and make a coffee date out of it. You can even challenge one other to "hack" each other to see how your security stacks up—together.

Protect your accounts

Informed consent is when you understand exactly what you're agreeing to, you have the power to decline, and you understand the consequences (as well as the benefits) of what you're agreeing to. It is the opposite of our relationships with just about every app, Internet company, and service that's tracking us and collecting our data right now. This crappy situation is a great reason for you to do a quick social media cleanup and tighten down the things you can control. This cleanup is also terrific in warding off trolls, stalkers, and other online pests.

First, log out of Facebook, LinkedIn, Twitter, Google+ and any other of your primary profiles, so you can see them as someone else would. Then one by one, view them and see what you don't want showing, and adjust your privacy settings accordingly. Don't panic if you see something you didn't realize was public, and don't blame yourself for what these companies have done to your privacy. What's online doesn't have to stay visible forever.

When you log back in to your account to adjust the privacy levels, pay attention to settings that control your visibility, what your profile looks like, what happens when you share photos on other sites, and who can see your photos or location. Pay attention to settings about who can tag your profile or photos, and shut off any "personalization" settings—this enables sites to share more data about you. Make a mental note for each site in regard to how you can remove your images, how to delete your profile, and get all location sharing settings reigned in so no one can find out where you are unless you want them to.

Step-by-step account security:

1. Sign out
2. Observe your accounts, take notes
3. Log back in and adjust settings
4. Review all privacy and security settings
5. Shut off location, disconnect apps you don't use
6. Turn on two-factor (2FA) password protection

Disable settings like *Suggest photos of me to friends* and *Friends can check me in to places*. Settings that automatically share things for you in the background can often spring unwanted surprises, such as telling someone where you are (or worse, where you live!) when you'd rather have privacy, or sharing embarrassing or revealing photos without your knowledge.

When you review what you've already shared, or if you're trying to decide what's safe to share before you press "upload" or "share" consider the following:

Photos and videos: When posting photos and videos, think about what you're doing in the image or video. Are you making protest signs with friends? Does the image reveal details about your home, work, credit card numbers, or vehicle? Is there a mailing address printed on an envelope?

Updates: When posting updates to your online profiles, choose how you want to share that content every time, whether that's publicly, with friends, or only with certain people. When posting, never share anything like your entire birth date, address, or phone number, or news about a trip you're going to take (i.e. that you'll be away from home).

Tagging: See who can tag you in a photo, post, check-in, or anything else where you'll be identified. Remember that tagging gives people the power to tell their friends—or the world—who you're friends with, where you are, what you're doing, or anything else. Restrict who you give this power to, if anyone.

Comments: When commenting on posts by others, pay attention to how you're posting. Are you posting with your real name? Does your comment reveal your name, location, or anything else that could be used to figure out private information?

Likes, upvotes, and favorites: When you click Facebook's Like button, upvote a post, or favorite something, that action will be reflected in your profile. Then visitors to the item you favorited may see your picture and a link to your profile.

Friending: Unless you really know and trust the person, don't. Yes, it looks cool to have a lot of friends. But all it takes is one troll to burn everything you've worked to protect. When friending someone, ask yourself why you're friending them. Do you actually know them? Do you trust them with your personal information or with access to details about your friends and family?

To harm, intimidate, and silence: Doxing

A common tactic used to silence people is "doxing." This is when an attacker or a group finds sensitive information on an individual (or individuals in a targeted group) and publishes it in a publicly accessible place online with the intent to do harm. The attacker usually encourages their own community and strangers to use the information for harassment and harm, and solicits the public for more information on the victims.

Information used to "dox" victims usually includes name, address, home/cell phone number, email address, workplace name and address, age, social media information, and sometimes race, sexual orientation, relatives, or more. It's then posted on forums, Pastebin, or other public locations. People who dox will think of creative ways to use the information for harm, and will find ways to bend the rules to do so. Once when I was doxed, the attacker posted my address on the Wikipedia page about me, which he maintains; he claimed it was in the public interest about me. The information was removed, but he was allowed to continue editing the page.

Most who dox will try to make it seem like they're hackers, or have special skills to hold over you. They're almost always not hackers, and what they're doing requires only access to the open internet.

In May 2017 Trump supporters from the Reddit group "/r/The_Donald" posted a document that doxed thousands of people who signed a public petition from the site Refuse Fascism (refusefascism.org), condemning the Trump administration. Buzzfeed traced the document to an April post on the 4chan messageboard. It contained all the usual information used in doxing, and also religious affiliation. The doc also listed the techniques with which members of the forum and subreddit used to find the victims' personal information.

Tips to defang doxing:

- Get your info off "people finder" sites.
- Make your domain registration info private.
- Do a social media cleanup to remove clues.
- Get a PO box; use it with everything you can.
- Use a "burner app" to obscure your phone number.
- Limit data sharing on Facebook, others.

The Trump supporters doxed their victims with publicly available info from Google, LinkedIn, Facebook, Twitter, and a "people finder" lookup site called Whitepages. On iTunes, the Whitepages app says, "Whitepages is the #1 and most trusted source for people & business search, with over 200 million U.S. households & businesses at your fingertips."

You can remove any listing you find about yourself on Whitepages by visiting this link: support.whitepages.com/hc/en-us/articles/203263794-Remove-my-listing-from-Whitepages-. There are many other sites like Whitepages, which as far as I'm concerned, are among the most reprehensible businesses in the world. Keep reading to find out how to get yourself off all these sites, and to obscure the data they use to create their nonconsensual profiles on us.

Get your personal info offline

"People finder" sites are indisputable tools of harm, and they're a big business powered by all that data collected on you by apps and internet companies. With a quick search of your name on any given people-finder site, you'll most likely find your name, date of birth, names of family members, current and past addresses, phone number, and gender. Some sites will also reveal your marital status, hobbies, online profiles, and maps or a photo of your house. Intelius, for instance, claims to offer over 100 "intelligence services," including a simple people search that provides a person's address and phone numbers and a background report showing criminal activity (though even Intelius conceded in a 2008 SEC filing that its information is often inaccurate and out-of-date).

Many people-finder sites will give up enough information about you for free to total strangers that finding out would make you choke on your latte. In other words, anyone with an Internet connection can stalk you from their couch with a couple dozen keystrokes.

Scary? Completely.

Take control of your private information right now. Find out what information is out there about you by searching for yourself. Searching for yourself might be daunting, even scary, and it might bring up negative feelings, but this is where you start getting tough on controlling your private property. Knowing is always better—and safer—than not knowing.

The first step to taking control is an online privacy check-up. Google your name using quotation marks, like "Mary Jones" (also check the Images tab). Google your phone number, home address, and Social Security number (tax ID). Don't panic if you find something online you didn't expect. From the results, make a list of "people finder" sites to contact and have your information removed.

You can fight this avenue of the privacy invasion business by opting out of people-finder websites. The opt-out procedures are often complicated and daunting, and they require you to go to each of the sites to request removal individually. If you can afford it, there are businesses that will do all the onerous work for you. Abine's DeleteMe service (abine.com/deleteme/landing.php) is excellent, and I highly recommend it. If you want to DIY it, the primary tentacles for all these sites are at the following addresses:

- BeenVerified (beenverified.com)
- DOBSearch: (dobsearch.com)
- Intelius: (intelius.com)
- LexisNexis: (lexisnexis.com/en-us/products/public-records.page)
- Spokeo: (spokeo.com)
- WhitePages: (whitepages.com)

Hack-proof your life

This may all seem quite overwhelming, but it's more manageable than it seems. Take action to make yourself safer online and more hack-proof than most people. In most instances it's as easy as changing a few habits.

Secure your device

There are different flavors of device security. One is general security: Things you set up for better everyday security and new habits that make you safer. Another is the kind of security steps you'll take when you take your device to a march, protest, or rally. Then there are the kind of security steps you'd take if you knew you were going into a digitally hostile environment, where you know you're going to be actively surveilled and attacked (like a hacker conference).

This section covers general device security. It's for use after you've learned about phone risks in Chapter 2, and tightened your settings. It's a step above what most people do, yet the changes are mostly just new habits and tips about avoiding getting hacked. Preparing your device for a protest or march, and further, is described in Chapter 9, "Taking it to the streets." Encrypted apps and VPN use are detailed in Chapter 5, "Defy Surveillance."

Two great guides to securing your device are at Let's Get Safe (letsgetsafe.org) and Digital Self-Defense in the Time of Trump (equalitylabs.org). Each have clear, easy to follow instructions. Let's Get Safe walks you through each device you have, and Digital Self-Defense has terrific one-sheet .pdf guides for phones, identity, network security, and more.

Start by activating the password lock on your phone, laptop, and tablet. This is critically important for many reasons. Yes, it's a hassle sometimes. But if your devices fall into someone else's hands, you'll be so glad you put up with this small inconvenience.

Just this little barrier will keep out the majority of crooks, stalkers, and authorities who might snatch your phone and try to see who your contacts are or read your email or texts. It won't keep out some hackers or authorities with resources to expend on using digital spy tools to get in, but it's a great stopping point for most adversaries.

It's important that you use a password wherever possible, and definitely not your fingerprint. A password, not a PIN number or fingerprint, is the only log-in method that's protected under law.

You can also be legally coerced or extrajudicially made to fingerprint-unlock your device. Judges and lawmakers are struggling to decide if a fingerprint and a password are the same thing in terms of your rights, and it would depend on where you are located and who took your phone or tablet to determine what your rights might be. Importantly, your fingerprint can be used to unlock your device without your consent, physically—police have done this in a few US states. You're better safe than sorry, so remember: Six digits are better than one.

Install a password manager. Password managers save all of your passwords safely in an encrypted vault. That way, you have them all in one place, no one can accidentally discover them, and you can make really complicated passwords, because the manager will keep track of them (and remember them) for you. You use one master password to unlock the password manager.

Use it on your computers, tablet, and phone to make tough passwords, and to fix any instances where you've re-used a password. Don't ever let your computer or your browser save (or "remember") your passwords. Never ever re-use a password on different sites, no matter how tempting it is. Use a password manager like 1Password, LastPass, KeePass, or any of the recommendations in the Resources.

One option for better security with phone calls is to mask your phone number, so it can't be used to find more information about you by malicious hackers. Get a free, Internet-based VoIP (Voice over Internet Protocol) phone number. Use it for any online communications. Don't worry—you can forward it.

This is helpful for keeping your risk of being hacked lower, and it's good when you want to set up separate online account identities that require a phone number. Google Voice isn't recommended because the company blends your separate accounts in the background, and I don't recommend Skype. I do recommend Hushed and CoverMe. Read more about buying and using burner phones in Chapter 4, "Your phone is a tracking device."

Reduce your attack surface

Your goal is to minimize all the places you can be attacked. The main way to do this is by strengthening your communication privacy, and getting your digital life as encrypted as possible. Read in-depth about encryption and PGP in Chapter 5, "Defy Surveillance."

Use two-factor authentication everywhere you can. Not all sites offer it, but two-factor (sometimes called 2FA) can protect your accounts from unauthorized access far better than just having a good password. Activate it everywhere that offers it. Once you've opted-in, you'll sign in like you ordinarily do, but there will be one extra step before you're allowed into your account.

Google and Amazon, for instance, will send a text message to your phone that has a short, randomly-generated numeric code that you'll need to enter to finish logging in. This means your phone is physically required for sign-in. Other companies will give you the option of getting the secondary code in a text message or email.

Never sign in on someone else's device or computer. Ever. When you do this you risk leaving your account information on their computer, should you forget to sign out, close the sessions, or clear cookies. There's also a risk of having your username and password stolen if the person has a program installed to record your keystrokes.

Use ad blockers like it's a religion. You can be hacked or infected with malware through ads, even on the biggest and most mainstream websites. That's because ad networks don't care about protecting the people who are seeing their clients' ads from being tracked, and they don't screen advertisers to keep out malicious content.

Install two or three anti-tracking (ad blocking) plug-ins and extensions in your browser. AdBlock Plus is good, but shouldn't be the only thing you use because it has a whitelist that allows paying advertisers to slip through the filter. uBlock Origin, Disconnect, and Abine's Blur are all great choices.

While you're at it, use a browser that cares about your security (and hopefully your privacy). Chrome's security is top of the line. For privacy, many people like the Brave browser, and Firefox.

Encrypt your computer's hard drive by enabling full-disk encryption in your settings. It will keep prying eyes out of your files should someone gain access to your computer or drive. Encryption lets you protect your electronic information with a virtually uncrackable password.

Search online to find out how to turn encryption on for your system. Look for Apple's built-in encryption program FileVault and BitLocker on Windows. Without encryption, anyone with a few minutes of access to your computer, tablet, or smartphone can spy on, copy, or steal your files, even if they don't have your password.

Back up everything. If you get infected with ransomware, a secure backup that's not connected to your network ensures you'll have all your data safe and sound, away from the affected machine. Ransomware is when you get hacked (usually by clicking on a bad link or viewing an infected website or ad) and all your files get locked up and held for ransom. Additionally, if you experience having your device confiscated or stolen, you can remote-wipe it without losing all your contacts or files. This is strongly recommended before you go to a march, protest, or event.

Tape over your webcam. It's remarkably, and unfortunately, easy to spy on someone through their computer, tablet, or phone's webcam. The programs used to do this is inexpensive, and don't turn on the little light by the camera, so you never know that they're recording. These kits are often packaged as child-tracking software. But that's not how they're used, and the results can be awful in the hands of creeps or authorities abusing their power. Stop this spying by putting a sticker, Post-It, or piece of tape over your built-in webcams. (This won't prevent audio spying.)

Before you hit the streets, make copies of your device's contacts, your files, and your photos. Make sure at least one of your backups isn't connected to your home network. You might consider backing up your files to a cloud service like Dropbox or Amazon, but if you do, make sure to separate that account from all other accounts by giving it a different username and password.

Use a secure backup hard drive that you keep at home (or in another safe place), or keep your backups on a computer that's separate from all others. CrashPlan is an example of a backup service that copies and stores your files on a regular schedule, and it also comes as stand-alone software. Apple's Time Capsule does it automatically for you, too.

Don't use a friend or family member's computer for backups because not only do you risk them looking at your stuff, but if they're compromised, your stuff is at risk, too. I like to back everything up into an external hard drive that I don't plug in unless I'm making the backup, and I keep it in my emergency earthquake escape bag.

Install an antitheft app. (Or activate "find my device.") An antitheft app like Prey or Lookout on your computer or phone gives you the power to track your devices and wipe them remotely if they get stolen or confiscated. With something like an iPhone, the only way most attackers can hack into your locked phone is to physically get their hands on it. Being able to erase all the phone's data and reset it puts control over your privacy back into your hands.

Antitheft apps usually camouflage themselves as games, if you set them to do so. They can show you where your device is on a map, take photos from the device's camera, and upload those photos to your online account. You'll be able to see where your laptop or phone is and who has it, so you can give this information to the police. These apps all do things a little differently, but the general idea is the same.

Don't click on strange links. Don't download unexpected attachments (files). The number one way people and businesses get hacked is through phishing. Phishing is a technique used to make you think that an email, SMS, or even a phone call is from a person, organization, or company that you trust.

They usually want to dupe you into disclosing your personal information or login credentials when you connect to what appears to be a legitimate website or data collection form. Phishing texts and emails may also trick you into downloading files or programs that contaminate your computer with malicious software.

When someone is trying to track or surveil you, they'll often get you to fall for a phishing email or text message with a link. Clicking a link sent in a text can open a link in your mobile browser, which in turn can install password-stealing malware on your phone just as it might on your computer. Mobile browsers are no more immune to phishing attacks than your desktop browser is.

Sometimes these links look surprisingly legitimate, like a real Google login page. Look closely at URLs if you consider clicking on them; often you can tell there's something wrong with the site address. If the URL is a link shortener (like a Bit.ly link, where people hide or obfuscate the final address destination) you should absolutely avoid clicking it. Some fake sites even display official-looking federal law enforcement symbols. One ransomware site even claimed to be the "Federal Internet Enforcement Administration" (which doesn't exist).

Keep an eye out for unusual account activity. Something is wrong if your accounts start sending password resets you know you didn't initiate or if you start getting account-recovery emails. Beware of account-recovery emails for accounts you know you didn't initiate. These are probably fake phishing emails designed to trick you into clicking links and entering your passwords, inadvertently revealing your information or allowing the installation of malware on your computer.

Consider getting a post office or business mailbox. You can use in place of your home address to minimize the risk of identity theft, stalking, and other dangers. Make your real address hard to find. If you have a website, make sure you have "WhoIs" privacy turned on. That's the option in a domain registration service's settings that shows your name and address as the registrant. Many people don't know that this information is shown to the public by default on website registration records, and can be easily found with what's called a "Whois" search. If the company your domain or website is registered with doesn't offer a "Whois" privacy feature, change registrars right away and hide that information.

Of course, you have to give real billing information when you buy things, but if you're registering with a free site that feels like it's getting too nosy about your business, give it fake information or your mailbox address.

Use different email addresses for different online accounts. You can set them up to forward email to the address you actually check. Different addresses will help you keep your separation of accounts in order, and won't make it easier for a company to try and merge your identities.

It's also a great way to keep track of spam and track any unusual behavior with an account. If you only use a specific email address with one account, you'll know exactly which account is being used for spam or attacks, because you'll receive email to that address. This technique is also handy should your account be in a mass hack and data dump; if everyone's login and passwords get put online, it'll only be the one address you need to do cleanup on. With less worry and minimal cleanup when there's a problem, you'll have more time to focus on being an agent of change.

CHAPTER 4

YOUR PHONE IS A TRACKING DEVICE

Our phones are a crucial part of who we are. In our hands constantly, they go everywhere we do. With them, we're connected to each other and the world, sending status updates, posting photos and videos, making our voices heard sometimes over and above the most powerful news outlets in the world. Cell phones are the digital revolutionary's most important tool.

It's important to point out that phone tracking isn't going to be a major issue for most people. Some people may be totally fine with authorities knowing where they are during something like a protest, especially for their own safety concerns if it becomes dangerous. However, it's important that you're fully aware just how much phones are being used to spy on us.

You should know that our phones are spying on us 24/7. These little handheld sidekicks are law enforcement and Big Brother's most useful asset when it comes to tracking and surveilling anyone. Greedy corporations can't believe how lucky they are to be around in the time of cell phones without strong privacy laws. Apps have permission to search your mail, meddle with your settings, scrape your address book, and even record you. Many apps share the information they get with marketers, data brokers, and authorities.

The only way we can completely refuse to be tracked is not to use our apps, or leave our phones at home.

But not using apps or going without a phone isn't a realistic option for anyone.

Smartphones leak your information and leave a trail of your information by design. Your info can be discovered and your habits known by any bystanders who know how to look. Hackers and developers have been trying to raise the alarm about phone security for years, but have gone practically ignored.

Every step you take, every place with Wi-Fi that you visit, and even friends who end up in your physical proximity, are revealed to anyone with a couple of bucks and the will to violate your life.

In 2016, a hacker in Bordeaux, France named Mehdi decided to see what he could learn about the people around him with a couple of off-the-shelf gadgets. What he found is unsettling and creepy. Over the course of six months he observed information leaking from people's devices while he was on his daily train commute, just through the Wi-Fi and Bluetooth data coming from their phones.

Mehdi found all this out without hacking into anyone's phone or planting hardware on them. He did it without a warrant, and with zero help from Apple or Google. Using a Raspberry Pi armed with a GPS, Wi-Fi and a Bluetooth sniffer, he created a lowbrow NSA-style phone tracking operation.

Whenever someone's Wi-Fi sent out probe requests for its home access points or their Bluetooth devices leaked information about what they were, he recorded it. The website HackADay wrote: "In the end, he got nearly 30,000 Wi-Fis logged, including 120,000 probes. Each reading is time-stamped and geolocated, and [Mehdi] presents a few of the results from querying the resulting database."

With this information, Mehdi tracked the entire commutes of

strangers. He saw when someone's phone sent out probes for a Domino's pizza Wi-Fi connection. Mehdi could even figure out "...which riders knew each other because they often connect to devices with unique IDs, which could be used to correlate them."

You can bet that every app you have installed is also slurping up this information, bundling it and selling it to advertisers.

We didn't sign up for this. We've been boxed into this privacy nightmare by our smartphones and their apps, which don't allow us to have a functional phone unless we formally agree to a legally binding Terms of Service.

For many hackers this is old news. In fact, InfoSec researchers have been raising the alarm by demonstrating how easy it is to play Mehdi's game of "capture the probe" for years. Malicious hackers and companies like Facebook alike consider such gaping security holes a feature to exploit for profit, not a flaw (though, of course, if it makes Facebook look bad, the company will trot out the usual "it's a bug" excuse).

At hacker conference DEF CON 21 in 2013, security researcher Brendan O'Connor presented a talk called "Stalking a City for Fun and Frivolity." His presentation was bracketed by some heavy emphasis on the fact that everything we use is leaking way too much data about us.

With tools O'Connor used, he recorded data and combined it to create a visualization "to show people with real faces and identities and histories moving around a map in 3D," he told *Computerworld*. "Even if you don't connect, if you are wired on a network, we will find you. If you are a person in a city, we will find you, and we will do it all for very little money."

The experiment, O'Connor explained, was to see how much data they could collect from local network traffic. "This means names, photos, services used, etc." It wasn't terribly difficult for him to make filters for grabbing data from specific apps, including "DropBox, Twitter, Facebook, and dating websites." He noted, "Now, many of these services encrypt their traffic, which is admirable." However, he added that in most instances "we can still get useful data that they provide in, e.g., their User Agent. And there's no reason for them to do this."

"This isn't even hard—and it should be hard. And that is pretty disturbing to me," O'Connor said. "People fix vulnerabilities when the kid on the street corner can abuse it. Maybe it's time to fix this now." Years later, we're no better off.

That talk was covered by a fair number of mainstream news outlets, and what O'Connor said has been repeated over the years in different ways by other security researchers. Still, it seems like most people don't realize what kind of data is being broadcast from their devices. Despite what appears to be consumers' growing concerns about privacy, 90% of people keep the location services function on their smartphones switched on at all times.

O'Connor soberly cautioned, "If every person on the planet can use this surveillance technology, I think we should start to design things not to leak information at every level. You leave behind a trail that can be tracked not just by the NSA or a law-enforcement agency, but by any kid in a basement with less than $500."

It may feel like there's no practical way to defy the built-in surveillance that phones provide. But I refuse to let phone and app makers show blatant disregard for the sanctity of our private lives. I won't give up the fight for privacy, or accept that it's "too late." And you shouldn't, either.

Keep reading this chapter to learn how to fight this. You'll make better decisions about the risks and rewards of including your cellphone in your everyday digital revolutionary kit.

The problem with phones at protests

Thanks to the 230 people who were arrested at the Trump inauguration protests, we are starting know more about how the authorities use phones against people who are arrested. In this instance, Washington, D.C. police swept up everyone they could. Medics, legal observers, and six journalists (*Voactiv*, *RT America*, others) were in the mass arrests. All of their phones were confiscated and retained.

One of the people arrested at the December 20 inauguration protests got an email shortly after the arrests from Facebook's "Law Enforcement Response Team" saying law enforcement wanted their data. In typical Facebook style, the letter was an inevitable countdown to that data being handed over unless the respondent figured out how to file an objection.

Everyone arrested in those protests now faces felony charges that carry penalties of up to 10 years in prison. In San Francisco, where we love a good protest, it's very rare that arrested protesters get prosecuted, so it's surprising for protestors to have their social media scrutinized after an arrest. As with most cities across America, the SFPD will commonly search the social media of suspects arrested if they believe that the suspect posted something related to the crime (like photos of a beating). SFPD even has an officer devoted to following social media—most heavily, Snapchat and Instagram, as those are apparently where you find the best evidence of crimes.

As for protests elsewhere in California, Oakland Police and other agencies like CHP haven't hid the fact that they are monitoring Twitter to determine protestor movement and plans. It makes sense that they're in the open about it, seeing that the Bay Area is ground zero for ethically challenged startups that invade our privacy. Fighting Big Brother's Silicon Valley BFFs has become part of our DNA. But a wide-ranging Facebook subpoena for felony protest prosecution isn't something we've seen the likes of—yet.

A subpoena issued to Facebook by the U.S. Attorney's Office on January 27, 2017, one week after the inauguration, requested by a D.C. Metropolitan Police detective, is chilling. Issued on yet a different inauguration arrestee, it requests subscriber information from Facebook that includes all names, all addresses (home, business, emails), phone records, session details (IP, ports, etc.), device identification info, payment information, and more.

"The redacted blocks on the second page shield columns of phone numbers, which are connected to other arrestees for whom the District Attorney and police are seeking information."

The list of phone numbers may indicate that police have gained access to someone's phone and are building a case with what they found. A screenshot provided to *The Atlantic's* webzine *CityLab* indicates police began mining information from the confiscated devices right after the arrests.

It's possible that any activity reporters and lawyers observed coming from the confiscated phone might've been something like automated pinging by Gmail to Google's servers. But consider this: When phones are taken as evidence, they're supposed to be secured in a signal-blocking Faraday bag to prevent remote wipes. Fred Jennings, a cybercrime defense attorney at the firm Tor Ekeland, P.C. in New York, told *CityLab* "If it had been secured properly and placed in the bag to safeguard it, there'd be no way for it to ping the server."

Less than six months after the arrests, court documents surfaced revealing efforts of the authorities to crack around 100 of the arrestees' phones to access the contents.

"The government is in the process of extracting information from the rioters' cellphones pursuant to lawfully issued search warrants, and expects to be in a position to produce all of the data from the searched rioter cellphones in the next several weeks," the filing read. The prosecutors also plan to try the accused en masse to save time, which you'd be inclined to believe is a violation of everyone's right to a fair trial, because it totally is.

It's interesting to note that the prosecutors were stymied by the simple act of locking a phone. "All of the rioter cellphones were locked," the filing said, "which requires more time-sensitive efforts to try and obtain the data." Keep in mind that it's the prosecutors who are stopped; forensic tools are certainly available for law enforcement techs to crack these phones.

It's not too much of a leap to worry that what happened to protesters in D.C. could happen to anyone who is in the wrong place at the wrong time—for example, during a peaceful march or protest that gets weird. Most people aren't being targeted by the CIA, FBI, or even the "collect it all, sort it out later" NSA—so unless you're committing a federal crime, government surveillance is probably not at the top of your personal "threat model." However, attending a Women's March or crossing an international border might put a variety of authorities on your list of possible surveillance threats.

This is essentially the online equivalent of the U.S. having a secret police cruising around everyday society looking for anybody saying anything suspicious.

It is also used in so-called "profiling" software, like the kind used by police in Los Angeles, California called PredPol (short for "predictive policing"). Not surprisingly, PredPol has been shown to unfairly target and profile African Americans for crimes the authorities believe people will commit.

Along with startups like PredPol, there are similar companies like Geofeedia who sell social media data to authorities for real-time surveillance. Geofeedia specifically marketed its service to police for targeting activists of color. It is one of over a dozen surveillance software systems marketed and sold to law enforcement around the country, and the world. They're used every day by police in departments across the U.S. Some combine all this with big data's profiles, bought and sold in volume thanks to the online advertising sector that companies like Facebook cater to.

For instance, the city of Denver, Colorado saw its police department spend around $30,000 on surveillance software designed to intercept, aggregate, and store social media posts across at least a dozen networks, according to police records. We found out when the Geofeedia story broke in 2016 that the company used social media sites' developer tools to monitor and collect people's posts, even if the posts are private.

With Geofeedia, Denver police acquired the ability to simultaneously monitor posts on Facebook, Twitter, YouTube, Instagram, Vine, Periscope, and Flickr, among others. Its location-based search capabilities enable police to vacuum up nearly every social media post emanating from within specified geographical boundaries. The tweets, photos, videos, and live broadcasts of anyone identified by the software within the area are intercepted and recorded by police through a process developers call "geofencing."

As you'd expect, this is a setup for abuse of power. It doesn't help that the big data profiles underlying many of these systems are based on incorrect information, leading to wrongful arrests. Basically, businesses are having a field day on selling data and access, while police and authorities are at an all-you-can-eat buffet of our data (so are advertisers, who are a huge part of the cycle). Lawmakers barely understand what's going on. So it's up to us to cut off as many avenues of surveillance possible, at the very least because absolutely no one is being responsible with our data.

Some of this could be solved by ditching our devices in favor of carrying on-the-scene burner phones, which is always an option (and described later in this chapter). But first, figure out what you can do to reduce your surveillance footprint with the phone you've got, because it may be all the protection you need.

Nail down your settings
Android, iPhone, Blackberry… You'll hear a lot of people telling you different things about what's safe and what's not. But what matters is that you know how to best use the phone you have, and find out

about any limitations in function, form, or in securing your privacy before you use it.

Most people use Android phones, though iPhones have advantages when it comes to security. That's not to say Androids can't be used securely, it means that iPhone has more control over their user's security—so you have less choice for ways to use your phone, and Apple has more control over you. Android has less control over your security, but it also comes with less limitation when you want to do something different, like use experimental apps.

Whatever phone you have, there are a few things you'll want to do to it while you're reading this chapter. We're going to do the basics in hack-proofing your phone.

First, grab your phone and set up a pass code or pin to unlock it, if you haven't already. Set it to time out with a duration that won't drive you nuts while you're using it, but also won't let a thief get into your phone if they snatch it out of your hands on the street. If you have Touch ID or fingerprint recognition, turn it off—your hand can be held to the phone to open it without your consent, which happens more often than you'd think.

Next, go into your phone's settings and look in the Security section. Turn on encryption. Spend some time in the Security settings, and change anything that you think might leave you exposed. Turn off Bluetooth and NFC if you're not using those features. Turn off anything that lets your phone connect to open (public) Wi-Fi on its own. You never know when you're connecting to a hostile network, so you don't want your phone randomly doing it without you knowing.

Device security 101:

- Activate a device password
- Turn on encryption
- Install and use a secure (encrypted) messaging service
- Install and use a VPN
- Keep your device and apps updated

Consider installing a VPN app on your phone for when you connect to public Wi-Fi, to protect your traffic from getting intercepted on those networks. Google's wireless data program Google Fi has automatic VPN built-in, so it detects when your phone is connecting to possibly insecure Wi-Fi, and protects you automatically. Read up on VPNs in the next chapter ("Defy Surveillance") and select one that works best for you: Any reputable VPN will have an app for your other devices. Use it whenever you connect to Wi-Fi.

Next you'll want to make sure no one can figure out your location when you take pictures with your phone. Most photo apps give you the option to remove the data that's in a photo file that can give snoops your exact coordinates when you took that photo.

On an Android phone, go to Settings and Apps, then tap each app you take photos with to see if it's collecting your location. Toggle Location to "off" if it isn't already.

To prevent your iPhone or iPad from saving location data in photos, you can follow these simple steps:

- Open up the Settings app.
- Navigate to Privacy > Location Services.

- You'll see a list of apps. Tap on Camera and then select Never.

Some apps will track your location in the background without your knowledge and send it to home servers in logs. Most phones allow users to toggle overall device location services on and off in Settings.

Phone signal interception

Just by the way it functions, a phone will routinely send your location to a base transceiver station, and records of your physical location will be stored in a database somewhere. It's not difficult to find (triangulate) where you are on a map even if you have location apps turned off, just by observing the cell towers and Wi-Fi hotspots your phone connects to. In extreme cases, there may be times when you need to leave your phone at home or somewhere else if you're really worried about being surveilled (or tracked by police at a protest, for instance).

Authorities are more frequently using fake base stations, also called "IMSI catchers" or "Stingrays" to track the location of citizens at protests and intercept their communications. They're used by police and federal government for what's called "lawful surveillance." The "lawful" part is up for debate according to digital civil liberties groups. In countries outside the U.S., this practice has been commonplace for quite some time.

In 2014, protesters in Kiev (Ukraine) who got close to the scene of violent clashes unexpectedly received a text message from authorities. It read, "Dear subscriber, you are registered as a participant in a mass riot." Afterward telephone providers MTS and Kyivstar both issued a statement saying neither had been responsible for sending out the messages. The texts came from law enforcement who had intercepted the cell signals of thousands of people, and wanted to discourage their further participation in protests.

Stingrays have entered our wider cultural discussions about authorities and surveillance, from protests to U.S. immigrant targeting. The ACLU discovered in May 2017 that Immigration and Customs Enforcement (ICW) and U.S. Customs and Border Protection obtained a search warrant authorizing use of a cell phone tracker to locate an immigrant suspected of being removable. "Although it has been publicly known for several years that ICE has purchased cell site simulator technology," ACLU wrote in a blog post, "this is the first time the ACLU has seen evidence of use of the technology in a particular ICE investigation or operation."

There is a lot of highly technical, frequently confusing, and often contradictory information about Stingrays and IMSI catchers. One of the pieces of advice you'll run into frequently online is that one symptom of IMSI (signal interception) use is noticing a fast battery drain on your phone.

However, it's also true that being in an area packed with lot of people using cell phones, or just doing a lot of photos, video, online status checks, or uploads will drain your battery just the same. If you're worried, keep your phone in "airplane" mode, or just shut off your phone. Turn it back on when you need it.

Ultra-cautious Android users will want to check out apps like SnoopSnitch (opensource.srlabs.de/projects/snoopsnitch). This app collects and analyzes mobile radio data to make you aware of your mobile network security. It warns about threats like fake base stations (IMSI catchers), user tracking, and red flags like unexpected, over-the-air updates.

If you're hungry for more technical knowledge, there are a few guides on cell phone knowledge and Stingrays/IMSI catchers listed in the "Resources" chapter.

Best phones to protect your data and best practices

No matter which phone you have, some company is Hoovering up your data and doing whatever they want with it. For Android, it's Google. With iPhone, it's Apple. Other phones may see you handing over your info to Microsoft, Blackberry, or others. Not all of them handle your data with equal respect to privacy and security, and each of them may (or may not) fight on your behalf against inquiries, requests, or demands from authorities to get your info.

Some are better at security than others; namely, Apple's iPhone. That extra bit of security comes with trade-offs, of course, such as Apple's censorship in its app store (limiting the revolutionary tools you can use on your phone), and other of Apple's issues. The iPhone, hands-down, has been the toughest for criminals to crack and the biggest pain for authorities who'd like to rifle through a user's digital belongings. That doesn't mean it's impossible to crack; no one phone is ever truly safe or secure.

Next in line for tight security is Google's own Project Fi network and the associated Android phones (Pixel and Nexus 6p), but this service isn't available everywhere.

Ultimately, you can counteract data collection, malicious hacking, potential government spying, and stalkers by following these best practices:

- Go into your phone settings and review all the privacy and security choices. Turn off anything you can that sends data back to Apple, Google, or anyone else—even if they say it helps improve your experience or their product.
- Look for ways to opt-out of data sharing with third parties: Search online for how to do this with both your phone system (like Apple) and your carrier (like AT&T).
- When you're in an environment you think might be digitally hostile, turn off Bluetooth and put your phone in "Airplane" mode until you need to use it.
- Don't let your phone join open Wi-Fi networks.
- Keep Bluetooth off to prevent hacking anyway.
- Never install an app you haven't researched to make sure it's safe first.
- Don't open texts or emails from anyone you don't know on your phone.
- Don't click links in texts or emails unless you have to, and only then from a person you trust. Same goes for opening attachments and images.
- Install and use a reputable VPN on your phone for when you need to use public Wi-Fi.
- Don't let your phone out of your sight, or let anyone else use it.
- Keep your phone PIN or password protected, and make it a good one.

- Be aware of anyone looking over your shoulder when you unlock your phone. Look out for cameras or phones that might be pointed at your screen.
- Avoid using the fingerprint unlock for your phone: it's legally less protected than your password or PIN. Also, your finger can be used to unlock the phone without your consent, and authorities have been reported doing this.
- Never charge your phone on an unfamiliar charger or cord; these can also be hacked, and it's not difficult.
- If you're going across a border, log out of your accounts.
- If you're going to an event like a march or protest, log out of all non-essential accounts. The essential ones would be the ones you're using to share the event (and media associated with it) and communicate with your group.

Burner phones and apps

A "burner phone" is just another name for a prepaid phone that's used in addition to (or sometimes instead of) your regular cellphone. A burner is usually bare-bones, and privacy-conscious people really like using burners for just that fact alone. You can buy a burner, or make your own. Typically, you'll buy a phone, or a phone plus a SIM card, and load up your burner with minutes.

Your burner can be a fully-functional, cheap, unlocked smartphone with a reloadable SIM card—perfect for keeping minimal personal info on, and taking with you to protests or across borders. It's your second phone. This way, your primary phone and all its information about you stays somewhere safe when you're in a tight spot.

Or, your burner can be a no-frills, no-apps, pseudononymous communication tool that makes it practically impossible to track you: Great for keeping you almost completely off the radar. One reason to go this route is to avoid carrying a device that has a Wi-Fi chip in it. In addition to apps tracking you, all tablets and smartphones come equipped with a Wi-Fi chip, which is one of the main ways you can be tracked and identified. The chip includes a unique identifier number known as a "MAC address." When your device connects to the Internet over Wi-Fi, the MAC address is reported and recorded.

Burners are great for privacy. When you buy one, you don't need a Google or iTunes account, GPS won't track your location, and you won't have ads in every app logging your activities. Prepaid carriers—like with the Ting SIM card—can't share your personal information because it's not collected unless you voluntarily give it to them. You can provide any name when you register your burner, or no name at all.

People get burners for a lot of different reasons. They're great to have as a backup if your phone dies. You can use them to avoid being tracked or spied on with your regular phone. Burners are hearty and can withstand being dropped, and you can use them with gloves because there's no touch screen.

It's important to know that burners can be legally traced, but it's just a lot more difficult. Burners can be tracked by using a method called cellular triangulation, which can divulge a fairly accurate location. But without anything else to tie it to (like a name or other data), it's not as useful to whoever is trying to spy on you.

One common kind of burner phone is the fully-functional Blu Phone, which can be found at in-person stores like Wal-Mart or

Target, or online at Amazon (among other places). If you buy a burner from Amazon, go pick up an Amazon gift card with cash at a retailer. TracPhone and Boost Mobile are other popular burners. Most are prepaid Android or Windows Phones.

If you want to restrict your surveillance footprint to its absolute minimum, all you need is an unlocked "GSM" phone (no apps or Wi-Fi) and a loadable SIM card. Be properly paranoid when you buy it; pay in cash for a gift card. Options for SIM cards include Ting, Zip SIM, GoPhone, Cricket, and others.

Start by popping the SIM card out of its package, and put it into your burner phone.

Now you're ready to activate the SIM card. Follow the instructions that came with the card, usually telling you to text in your zip code. A few minutes later, you'll get a text message back with your new local phone number. You're ready to go!

You might be wondering, what's the point of a digital revolutionary using a phone if it doesn't have apps for sharing and communicating? Guess what: Even if your burner phone only has SMS, you can still communicate with apps and social networks. This gives you a way to make updates without Internet service. It'll also mean little-to-no tracking of your location and activities, plus you're not losing the farm if your phone gets dropped or confiscated.

It's easy to set up SMS access for Twitter and Facebook. Sign into Twitter in a browser window, and navigate to the mobile options page. Follow the steps to add your new burner phone's number to your account, and then you're all set to send and receive updates by text. Keep in mind that you'll want to save on prepaid minutes, so only subscribe to essential Twitter alerts (like direct messages or mentions). Once you're set up, learn the short list of commands you can use with SMS and you'll be able to use Twitter on your burner. Then, just text 40404 to send out a tweet.

For Facebook, log in and visit your mobile settings page. Follow the directions to add your new burner number, then you'll be able to send and receive texts for new messages. After setup, you can text FBOOK (32665) to update your status.

One interesting option are apps that act as a burner number on your phone (some work with iPad). These app anonymize your texts and phone calls by routing your call or message through a new phone number. It's an actual phone number that works, so you can give that number out to people without revealing your identity. If you want to "burn" and discard that number, just delete the number and it'll go out of service. You can also use them as a kind of caller ID, to keep your real number private.

The Burner app is $4.99 a month, and is available for iOS and Android devices. Burner has a Chrome extension that helps with managing numbers, but it doesn't do calls or texts on the desktop. It does, however, integrate with apps like Dropbox, Evernote, Slack, and SoundCloud to help you with sharing or storing voicemails and contacts. Burner also lets you lock it with a PIN code.

Hushed is similar to Burner. It starts with a five-day free trial, then $1.99 for seven days or $3.99 per month with limited calls and texts. Hushed will become VoIP, meaning it'll default to making calls over Wi-Fi when it can, rather than using data. All texts between Hushed users are free, and they "disappear" (auto-delete after being read. Unlike Burner, Hushed is available in over 40 countries. It comes in iOS and Android flavors.

CoverMe, another burner app, has end-to-end encryption for conversations between CoverMe users, including calls and texts made over phone numbers provided by the company. They don't like to be called a "burner app" though, preferring to say the provide a secure virtual phone system. Everything with this app stays in a password-protected, encrypted vault. You can send self-destructing messages, and remotely wipe messages you've sent. It has a lot of security features, like decoy passwords. CoverMe is available for Android and iOS, and starts at $4.99 for a basic package.

Finally, you can take complete control over your phone by making your own. Read how in Chapter 6, "Gear Up."

CHAPTER 5

DEFY SURVEILLANCE

The amount of surveillance we're under from corporations and authorities alike should be worrying to anyone, regardless of your politics. Spying on us is big business.

Internet companies have reshaped the world into an economic system dependent on monetizing the ways they can track and surveil us. Then they try to smooth it over with doublespeak about "improving our experience" or "keeping our communities safer." In just one example, smart TV company Vizio had to pay $2.2 million in 2017 to the FTC for its unprecedented spying on customers. Facebook has been an arrogant foe of privacy advocates since it launched, and its data coffers fuel surveillance by authorities. In 2016 the company announced its plans to track which physical stores people shop at and report that information to advertisers. Where do you think that information ends up? Everywhere developers want it to be.

We're out of bounds with spying on each other, as well. Surveilling each other with the use of apps has been happening for as long as consumers have had tech in their homes. In 2017 two commercial cellphone surveillance products, FlexiSpy and Retina-X, were hacked revealing that everyone was spying on someone; parents, construction workers, lawyers, jealous lovers, and more.

Authorities are routinely overreaching with surveillance too, regardless of the law. In a 2016 oversight report, we found out that warrantless spying on Americans had more than doubled since the NSA disclosures of 2013. In 2015, New York police were caught lying about the use of Stingrays to intercept citizens' phone signals, doing so without court oversight.

Politicians see it as their duty to actively help those they think matter most--the wealthy and powerful people, corporations, and countries. Coming full circle back to 2017, this is the year the White House made it free and legal for our internet service providers (ISPs) to track, record and sell all the information they can grab about our online habits.

Defying surveillance isn't about being a liberal, conservative, socialist, or anarchist. It's about standing up for our rights to keep our personal information and our secrets private, and to insist on consent. You need to communicate safely and learn how to defy surveillance every day, whether you're gearing up for a rally, keeping your parents out of your personal life, or angry as hell about corporations and cops stepping all over your rights.

If you skipped Chapter 3 ("Hack-proof your life") and Chapter 4 ("Your phone is a tracking device") then skip right back and read those first. Then you'll be ready for the next level: Anonymity and encryption.

Keep your communication private

When you want to message friends and family but want to make sure your communication isn't being spied on, you'll want to avoid regular SMS (text messages) and apps like WeChat or Snapchat. That's because neither of these messaging methods use what's called "end-to-end encryption."

Think of end-to-end encryption as if you're sending your messages in a sealed canister, where only the outside of the container is seen by anyone except your recipient. At various points in its journey, the canister is checked to make sure it's sealed, and it verifies its identity. The only person that can open it is the person you send it to. The companies handling your message can't see it or open it.

Encrypted apps

Encryption is complicated to set up and maintain if you're not technical, so it's not the kind of thing you can necessarily do yourself. Fortunately more apps are using it than ever before, so you just need to pick the right one.

For most people, apps like WhatsApp, Facebook Messenger, and Signal (Open Whisper Systems) will do the job nicely. They each have drawbacks. Both WhatsApp and Messenger are owned by Facebook. The company has been pretty obvious about the fact that it scans the content of communications in Messenger, and have been facing some legal heat over it. If you use Messenger, be sure to turn on "Secret Conversations" to activate encryption.

As of this book's publication, a German consumer group is suing Facebook over its decision to link and track users' profiles between the two services (it matches your WhatsApp account with your Facebook profile) to gather more data for its advertisers.

Signal, which comes in phone and desktop versions, is seen as safer and more secure than the Facebook owned alternatives. Yet Signal has a few drawbacks, too. At this time, there is no way to hide your phone number within the service—so anyone you communicate with on Signal will see your phone number. In one instance, it led to the unmasking of a once-anonymous source that insisted on communicating with journalists over Signal. The press outlet found out who the source was by Googling their phone number.

Signal notifies your contacts when you install (join) the service by sending Signal messages to your contacts announcing your arrival—only if those contacts use Signal. You can't turn off that message being sent, you don't get a notification that it was sent, and you aren't told whom it goes to. So if you don't know who uses Signal in your address book, you may want to hold off until Signal (hopefully) creates the ability to make it anonymous.

One app that gets it all right is Threema. With this app, you can be as anonymous as you like, and it gives you fine-grain control over who knows you're on the service, or not. You don't have to let it scan your contacts, and you can create a random profile username, among many other great details. Telegram is another popular encrypted app, but many hackers and security professionals don't trust it. If you use it, be sure to turn on encryption and know that it doesn't work on group messages.

VPNs and online anonymity

Websites and their advertisers are continually making a record of your unique IP address and tracking what computer or cell phone you're coming from. This means they have a very good idea of your physical location. They could also stitch together information about your online activity. In worst-case scenarios, authorities can contact your Internet Service Provider (ISP) and obtain your identity.

If all that is something you want to keep private, you should know that you can't trust these businesses (and probably not their employees) with that information. You'll need to decide if it is important for you to hide your IP address when you visit certain websites or during certain activities or time periods.

Most people prefer to only protect their IP address when they're using Wi-Fi or Internet access they don't know or trust. Some people are careful to hide their IP address when they use their laptops in public, like at a café (it helps safeguard against malicious hackers), but they don't bother to hide their IP at home on their own network. Some people don't mind if their IP address/location is known to websites and their partner businesses. Others find that trying to keep their IP address private is such a pain in the ass that they make peace with taking the risk.

If there was a show on Netflix about stealing candy from babies, it would look a lot like using public Wi-Fi without a VPN. All advice about attending (or getting anywhere near) a hacker conference begins with "Get a good VPN for all your devices and use it at all times." Turns out there are some scary-good reasons for that.

A VPN, or virtual private network, masks your computer's IP address. You can use a VPN to secure access to your own network as well as to public Wi-Fi or Internet access spots. It's a great way to keep your browsing private, your IP secret, and you attack-proof. A VPN is also a handy way to protect your identity if you want to leave a comment or browse secretly without the website you're visiting knowing your location.

In companies, a VPN is typically used to connect employees who aren't at the workplace to a computer at work; they connect remote employees to central work servers. Many companies have VPNs so workers can access files and other resources over the Internet. Outside of company use, VPNs are being used more and more by people who just want to make their Internet use more secure from attackers.

Using a VPN might feel like insider InfoSec knowledge at this point, but so was making complex passwords not too long ago. When you use a VPN, the only thing an attacker sees is your computer talking to it—they can't see the connection to the sites you're visiting. Your Internet connection travels encrypted from computer to VPN server; from there the user's connection travels unencrypted to their final destination (a website). This way, websites only see the VPN's IP address and not yours. The ability of anyone to spy, intercept, attack, or steal information stops at the VPN.

When you use public Wi-Fi in a café, plane, or airport without turning on a VPN first, you can be hacked by anyone who's downloaded any of the many, excellent, free, open-source network traffic analysis tools (like Wireshark or TCPDump). The risk of being scanned like this is typically low in private networks, and extremely high in public ones.

Without a VPN, someone with one of these tools who is on the same network as you can see the URLs you're looking at, metadata, and any information transmitted between you and the sites you're visiting. They can also maliciously inject traffic, where you visit a trusted web page that's spiked with code to infect you with malware, which typically steals your banking and identity credentials.

Even if the connection is encrypted (yet you're sans VPN), the attacker is limited to the URL you're visiting and any leaking metadata. But if it's not an "https" site, they'll be able to see and capture plain-text passwords.

If you turn off your VPN to watch Netflix, and leave browser tabs or online apps with active sessions running in the background, you're handing over to malicious hackers anything that's being transmitted while you're watching Netflix.

How to install a VPN:

1. Choose a reputable service
2. Sign up/subscribe
3. Install it on all your devices
4. Adjust your settings
5. Open and surf!

Once installed, a VPN is simple to use: just turn it on before you go online (before you open your email, open a browser window, and so on), and you're all set. In a public Wi-Fi environment like a café or airport, you'll need to log in to the Wi-Fi first and then open your VPN before making another move.

I love how much better I feel using a VPN when I'm at hacker conferences! I can't imagine life without using a VPN, and I can't recommend VPN use strongly enough.

Find a safe VPN

Selecting a VPN you can trust already took research and consideration, weighing connection speeds and pricing, learning about who keeps records and for how long and more. VPN services are also like any other in that they change their record-keeping policies and privacy practices over time, so that's another thing to keep up with.

In addition, these services can accidentally be misconfigured by the VPN itself. Just over a year ago, VPN provider Perfect Privacy found a massive security hole in many services called "Port Fail." It was a bug that de-anonymized users, and most VPN services ignored the problem until the press made noise about it. Many took weeks to put in a fix. One of those was a service endorsed by Lifehacker, which just shows that anyone can have problems finding a reputable VPN.

It can be overwhelming. It's not as simple as using whatever VPN the security cool kids say is "the one," because even popular services have been behaving badly. For example, popular service Hola VPN recently got caught selling user traffic to a botnet.

Fortunately like most InfoSec topics, VPNs are a bit of a fetish unto themselves for people who are into them. If you want to know what the hallmarks of a trustworthy VPN service are, I have a controversial suggestion for you: the website Torrent Freak. Every year the site writes a post asking, "Which VPN Services Take Your Anonymity Seriously?"

In these extensive posts, TF talks to dozens of top VPN services and asks them what their record keeping policies are, as well as "various other privacy related issues." If a VPN gets a great review one year, has a less great review the next, and then drops off the list completely (like TigerVPN did), then definitely take that as a "buyer beware."

So if a VPN is recommended somewhere, do a little homework before you fork over your data (and your cash). Names that come up as trusted include Perfect Privacy, Freedome, TorGuard, Tunnelbear, FoxyProxy, Black VPN and others. It's generally considered best to use a paid (rather than free) VPN service, and there are a lot of great inexpensive ones to choose from. Your home Internet service provider might even offer a reputable one for free.

Should you have one for your phone? Absolutely, and most VPNs have mobile apps—though look out for the bad ones. Google's Project Fi (the company's phone service provider) automatically secures users on a Google VPN in every public Wi-Fi situation.

The drawbacks? They can slow your connection down, and they may not work with services like Netflix that want to know where you're physically located. Some public places block the use of VPNs, which should be your sign that the network isn't safe to use anyway.

Once you're all set up with your new VPN, use the steps in this post on Lifehacker (lifehacker.com/how-to-see-if-your-vpn-is-leaking-your-ip-address-and-1685180082) to test your VPN to make sure the outside world can only see your VPN's IP address, and make sure you're not leaking your actual IP. Another recommended (and reputable) tool to try is Cocoon. Cocoon hides your IP address when you access the Internet with a Cocoon account, and the Cocoon client can be installed on your browser or on your mobile device.

Tor is one option

One way to protect your identity as you cruise around the Internet is to use the free Tor ("The Onion Router") tool or apps that use Tor, like Orbot for Android. Tor is software that allows users to browse the Internet anonymously—most of the time.

Tor is often recommended for dealing with totalitarian regimes and targeted surveillance, rather than people who want to prevent getting hacked or surveilled on public Wi-Fi, want to use torrents, or want to hide their IP address. When it's time to undertake sensitive tasks online, it's best to have several privacy and security options at your disposal rather than automatically turning to Tor.

You certainly wouldn't want to use Tor for everyday browsing. Bouncing traffic between relays will considerably slow down your internetting. If you're uploading or downloading media for an event or are in the middle of developing news (like a protest), you'll need to be very patient.

It is not easy to set up (or troubleshoot) if you're not particularly tech-savvy. As the Tor Project notes, it "does not protect all of your computer's Internet traffic when you run it. Tor only protects your applications that are properly configured to send their Internet traffic through Tor." They add, "To avoid problems with Tor configuration, we strongly recommend you use the Tor Browser."

How to install Tor:

- Download the Tor Browser Bundle (torproject.org/projects/torbrowser.html.en)
- Double-click to extract the folder
- Open it and click "Start Tor Browser"

- Decide where to keep it
- Click "Install"

When Tor sends your traffic bouncing around through different relays, it eventually comes out through a single one before sending you to your final destination. The last relay is called the "exit node." Because Tor doesn't encrypt your traffic between an exit node and the destination server, any exit node is in a position to intercept any traffic passing through it.

An example of what this can mean happened in 2007 when a security researcher intercepted thousands of emails sent by human rights groups by surveilling the connections coming out of an exit node he was running.

This problem can be solved by using end-to-end encryption on everything while you're using Tor.

Take extra care opening files downloaded via Tor, as they may access the Internet behind the scenes and give away your true IP address. Digital Rights Management (DRM)-protected media files can be used to reveal Tor Browser users' actual IP address and therefore possibly reveal their identity. If your situation is truly dire, do your research to ensure that you're not vulnerable to threats like DNS leaks and attacks designed to cross-reference your Tor activities with your non-Tor activities to track you down.

If you only want to stop websites and advertisers tracking you online then hardening your browser with plugins like Privacy Badger or NoScript will do the trick without drawing attention to yourself. If you're not concerned about anonymity but simply want to stop people eavesdropping on sensitive information, then secure HTTPS connections and/or a VPN should keep your secrets safe.

Likewise, if you're primarily concerned about the metadata retention scheme but have nothing significant to hide, then Tor is overkill. A correctly configured VPN should be enough to mask your IP address, so efforts to track online activities back to you come to a dead end.

What if I'm paranoid?

The most complete way to go to blocked sites and avoid Internet surveillance is to use an operating system called "Tails" (or The Amnesic Incognito Live System). Like the Apple, Windows, or Android operating systems, Tails is an environment within your computer that you switch to using instead of your computer's regular operating system. It forces all outgoing connections through Tor, and non-anonymous connections are blocked.

The Tails website (tails.boum.org) explains you can:

- Use the Internet anonymously and circumvent censorship;
- All connections to the Internet are forced to go through the Tor network;
- Leave no trace on the computer you are using unless you ask it explicitly;
- Use state-of-the-art cryptographic tools to encrypt your files, emails and instant messaging.

Like Tor, Tails is not a "silver bullet" against spying or getting around censorship. A "Warning" page on the Tails website explains what Tails doesn't protect you from, including user missteps and certain kinds of targeted attacks. For instance, it won't protect you from compromised hardware, firmware exploits, man-in-the-middle (MiTM) attacks, or being targeted by a global adversary.

Your Internet Service Provider (ISP) or your local network will see that you're connecting to a Tor relay, so be cautious about drawing attention by using Tails. It also doesn't protect you form yourself, meaning that it won't remove metadata in documents or photos, nor will it separate your identities. To keep identities separate while using Tails, only use one identity at a time and shut down/restart Tails when you switch identities.

Tails can be installed and run on a DVD, USB stick, external drive, or SD card. Once you turn off your computer (or in case of danger, just unplug the USB stick), your Internet activity and disappears without leaving a trace, not even on the external drive. Conveniently, Tails has a great setup assistant on its website that walks you through the installation process (tails.boum.org/install/index.en.html).

Encryption and PGP

When the U.S. government's widespread surveillance by the National Security Agency (NSA) was revealed through leaks in 2013, most people learned that governments can spy on anything they want to. And when government authorities fail at spying on us, they make private companies hand over information about users.

It's no longer a matter of finding a microphone in a lampshade; we seldom know we're being tracked. In fact, companies like Facebook, Yahoo!, Microsoft, and others have been pretty up front about the fact that this happens every day.

Company employees and agencies like the NSA also do bad things for their own purposes all the time. In 2013, U.S. officials confirmed to the Wall Street Journal that NSA officers and employees used the agency's eavesdropping tools to spy on their love interests. The practice has a typical NSA spy-ops name: LOVEINT, short for love interest.

It's enough to make anyone want to have truly private communication, regardless of whether or not you want to join a protest. You can protect your email, instant messaging, texting, and Internet browsing from attacks like these, and more, when you start adding encryption to your digital life.

Without encryption, anyone with a few minutes of access to your computer, tablet, or smartphone can spy on, copy, or steal your files.

Encrypting your computer lets you protect your files with a virtually uncrackable password, and Windows, Mac, iOS, and Android all offer ways to encrypt your local storage. Search online to find out how to turn encryption on for your system. Look for Apple's built-in encryption program FileVault and BitLocker on Windows.

That takes care of your startup drive, but what if you have other drives or files? Locking a folder is a simple barrier that puts a basic level of protection on your files, but encrypting the folder is much better if you really want to keep it private—this process uses a cipher to make the data contained within completely unreadable, so it can't be circumvented as easily. Multiple internal drives, partitions on a single drive, external drives or thumb drives are not included in FileVault or BitLocker, so if you want to encrypt those you have to do it manually.

When it comes to email, there are a range of ways to secure what you send and receive.

When selecting an email provider, choose a major company that offers web-based email, and make sure it uses Secure Sockets Layer (SSL) to send email securely. SSL establishes an encrypted link between a web server and a browser, creating a secure connection. You can tell when a website uses SSL because the address bar (where the URL appears) will show https instead of http.

If an email service (or website in general) doesn't use SSL, it's not taking your security seriously at all. So if you fill out a form, press Submit, and the website doesn't have the s, it means that attackers could read all the information you just submitted to the website. If instead the website is using https, the information being sent over the Internet is encrypted, and it can't be read by anyone snooping on Wi-Fi—or any network—traffic. Needless to say, you should never ever enter your credit card number into a website that only uses http.

I recommend installing the plug-ins and extension HTTPS Everywhere, which turns your browser into a privacy shield by enabling encryption automatically on sites that support it.

You can take it further. The only way to truly, 100 percent keep your email private is to use something called OpenPGP. This is email encryption, which protects your email so that the only person who can read it is the one you're sending it to. (PGP stands for "pretty good privacy.") There are a couple of free options that aren't prohibitively technical, such as Mailvelope and GPG Suite.

GPG Suite is an open source (Mac only) plugin for Apple Mail that's incredibly easy to install and use. With a few simple clicks, you can encrypt, decrypt, sign and verify email.

You can purchase commercial PGP software or use free plugins like Mailvelope. If you're more technically inclined, download the open source version that uses the OpenPGP protocol, such as GPG (GNU Privacy Guard). No matter what, if you want to send an encrypted email, you need your recipient's public key (if they have one).

Many PGP implementations have plug-ins for different email clients, such as Outlook on PCs or Mail on Apple computers. As with all software, this can be problematic when system updates and PGP implementation updates don't come at the same time. Also, it's important to note that you might be restricted from using PGP at work or on your employer's network.

With free services such as Mailvelope, any recipient you send an encrypted message to will have to enter a password to read it—and without the password, your message will just look like a bunch of garbage. Gmail/Google Apps, Outlook, Yahoo!, and GMX are all supported, and the app can be configured to support others.

Mailvelope is a browser extension for Google, Chrome, and Firefox that allows secure email communication based on the OpenPGP encryption standard. The framework of Mailvelope and products like it is relatively straightforward. First, install the plug-in. Next, you'll generate a key pair, which means you'll use the plug-in to make two sets of code. One set is called your public key, and this is the one you'll publish. Each contact in your address book who uses PGP or products like Mailvelope will have their own public key, too.

The next time you open Gmail, Yahoo!, or whichever email brand you use, you should notice a lock icon in the compose area when you begin an email. When you're done writing and ready to send, just click on the lock icon, and Mailvelope should encrypt the message with the recipient's public key (if they have one) when you hit send.

When you get an email that's encrypted, the process goes in reverse. You should see the encrypted message with a lock on it, so just click it to enter your key as a password to open it. Mailvelope will then search your saved keys to find the right one and decrypt the message for you.

You have a few options when it comes to encrypted chat apps. Signal is considered the best choice by far, with iPhone, Android, and desktop versions. With Signal you can also make encrypted phone calls. iMessage is for Apple iOS only, but it's a great choice.

WhatsApp is another popular choice, and it runs on Signal's secure protocol—though it is owned by Facebook. WhatsApp updated its terms of service in August 2016 to begin sharing names and phone numbers with its parent company, Facebook--which is under investigation for lying about automatically matching WhatsApp users to their Facebook profiles when it acquired WhatsApp in 2014. One app to flat-out avoid is Telegram, which has a laundry list of security problems.

There's another way keep your online messaging secure: A tool called Off-the-Record (OTR) messaging. OTR encrypts your instant messages when you use services like Google Hangouts and Facebook Chat.

Chat/IM software clients like Adium and Xabber all come with OTR messaging, and there are OTR plug-ins you can get if you use clients like Pidgin. OTR encrypts your messages so they can't be read if someone intercepts them, but it doesn't let you save your chats—which might be a desirable thing, depending on how private you want to make your communication. Using OTR means that even the service sending and receiving your IMs and chat can't read the content.

Although it's the best tool we have today, PGP encryption (and OTR) isn't bulletproof. If the NSA really wants to spy on you, it has the resources to figure out a way to break OTR (if it hasn't already). But that takes money, time, staff and a really good reason. Unless you're hiding state secrets or doing something really nefarious that will make the authorities hunt you down, PGP and OTR should do the job for you, because you probably care more about keeping your messages confidential than about evading authorities.

It's important to also consider that there are ways for people interested in digging up dirt on you to use information that PGP doesn't encrypt. Like the recipient of your message, when you messaged them, their IP address, and so on. That said, if you're an activist (or journalist, blogger, or writer) in a country where you're a government target, use encrypted communications with caution. Reports of activists "flagged" for targeting because they use encryption (or privacy tools such as Tor) are not uncommon.

Like everything in privacy and security, it pays to be cautious and slightly paranoid. Still, it's easy to get caught up in surveillance hysteria, or feel like an outsider when limelight-addicted activists one-up each other about who knows more, or has better "OPSEC" (shorthand for "operational security"). Ignore the hype and posturing, and listen to your gut. Fighting surveillance is a very personal experience, and unique to each person's situation and needs. Take what you've learned in this chapter, its tools and information, and assess what's best for you.

CHAPTER 6
GEAR UP

There's an unbelievable amount of versatile gear to help you document and share your experiences in creating change. Cellphones, wearable body cameras, security gadgets, and more are readily available to take your resisting to the next level. Yet even the best gear doesn't always do what we need it to, and there are items you can create that surpass anything you can buy.

In this chapter you'll find out how to make your phone a better tool, and how to pick the best gear. You'll also find out how to make an open source protest sign that can call a lawyer for you if confiscated, and a mobile library of "know your rights" documents anyone can access.

Phone prep

Your phone is your most important piece of gear. Every digital revolutionary needs her phone, locked down for security and ready to connect to the world. But that's not where your gear list ends because there are other gadgets you'll want (and need) in your revolutionary go-bag.

Get your phone ready for action. Make sure you read Chapter 4 ("Your phone is a tracking device") so you know how to tweak your phone to minimize its ability to snitch on you. After that, the basics of phone prep are:

- Back up your address book and all files.
- Activate "Find my phone."
- Sign out of every app you won't be using.
- Make sure your password is on.

Do a little inventory of the apps you use for taking photos, recording video, posting status updates, and communicating with your community. Make sure they're easy to access. Some phones will let you assign a key or make a shortcut for taking photos or video; set that up so you're always ready.

Media use can drain your battery faster than you expect. So can using Wi-Fi when there are a lot of people around (among other things). Consider getting a small extra battery pack to stash in your bag so you don't run out of juice at the moment you need it the most. There are lots of inexpensive, slim, and light "juice packs" you can get that won't add a lot to your load.

If you're going to be out and about, you may want to do a little DIY work on your phone and attach a wrist strap to it. This way, if you phone gets knocked out of your hands, you won't lose it. Buy an inexpensive case on Amazon, and salvage or buy a small camera wrist strap—the kind that is just a cord. Then you can do one of two things. Before you snap the case on, attach the wrist strap through one of the case's available holes.

Snap it on and test it (over your bed or something soft). If the case doesn't fit snugly enough for you, there's another option: Drilling a tiny hole in the bottom right corner of the phone case. This won't massively harm the integrity of your case, and it's a solid option. I've had my phone on a wrist strap in this fashion for years; the latest version has lasted for the year I've had my phone (and still going).

Make your own burner phone

In Chapter 4, "Your phone is a tracking device," you'll learn all about "burner" phones and "burner apps" that reduce your surveillance footprint. You'll also read about what to consider when bringing your phone to a rally, march, or protest. Read it so you can do a risk assessment about surveillance in public places and what happens if you lose your phone.

So often, our tech choices make us feel like we don't have control. This is especially true when it comes to our phone—a source of both joy and powerlessness. It just feels so wrong that our phones are tracking devices we pay for, but we can't do anything to open them up and change them. But guess what? You can actually make your own phone. It's a great choice if you're a bit handy and buying a burner phone or using a "burner app" isn't for you. As with a real burner, you won't be able to check Facebook from a DIY handset, but you'll have control over everything—including your data.

All it takes is buying parts (around $150 total), learning a few hardware hacker skills to put it together, and then getting a refillable SIM card. (A Ting SIM typically costs $9.) Making your own phone reduces your surveillance footprint to just about zero, and it's completely legal.

The easiest, cheapest and most complete tutorials on making your own phone are on Adafruit.com, where they also sell kits and a cheap 2G SIM card—everything you need in one spot. This project doesn't require a lot of parts. With Adafruit's libraries, you can make your own touch-screen dialer in just 200 lines of code.

Learning to build a little phone that makes and receives calls (as well as SMS) will explode your gadget powers. You can make it as simple or complex as you like; if you're technical, design your own interface or code up a custom app. When you program it, you can have it do things like call 911 when you send it commands. Attach it to your open source protest sign and you've got something that can send out messages or calls if the sign gets confiscated, or if there's trouble at an event.

To get started look for Adafruit's Arduin-o-Phone, the Adafruit FONA, and a Ting SIM card. Direct links to tutorials and parts are in the "Digital Revolutionary Project Guide" chapter.

Body cameras, point and shoots

For some people, their phone is all they need when it comes to capturing and sharing photos and video. That's great for traveling light—but you only have two hands, and your phone camera isn't always that great.

Body cameras take the pressure off when you want to keep your hands free to tweet, text, or just put the need to document everything on automatic pilot. These "action cameras" that clip to a hat, a body harness, or strap to tour belt or wrist can also come in handy when you're at an event that might need to be streamed, or gets disputed later. They're especially helpful if you're following advice from the Indivisible Guide for meeting with congressional representatives, which is to "record everything."

It's important to remember that they turn you into a walking surveillance device, so use caution about other people's need for privacy and consent, and know your rights about taking videos and photos in public (versus private) spaces.

Action cams are designed to be attached to helmets, sporting equipment, cars and other objects, and they're small, tough, and easy to use. GoPro is the name everyone recognizes, with their well-known boxy Hero cameras. Action cameras also come in different prices, specialties, and styles, like a "bullet" shape. Other names to look for include the TomTom Bandit, Garmin Virb, Drift Stealth, Sony FDR-X1000V, and the iSAW Edge.

A body-mounted action camera isn't just for video. You can set it to take a photo every second, ten seconds, or sixty seconds. You can also livestream from most of them, but if that's your main goal, you should do a little research before your buy to make sure your current setup is compatible with livestreaming services. For instance, GoPro's Hero connects through its app to Periscope, but doesn't work with Facebook Live.

If you want to grab video or pics from the perspective of what you're seeing, a head or helmet mount is what you want. Something like GoPro's Head Strap and a QuickClip will do the job, and just the clip will let you put the camera on a hat, belt, or more. Helmet mounts come in different configurations; just make sure your helmet and the camera are compatible. Most helmet mounts will stick on your helmet with a powerful adhesive. Your camera can go on the front, back, or side, depending on what works best for you.

A chest harness is nice when you want to keep the camera view steady, forward, and difficult to jostle or knock loose. Straps like criss-cross suspenders place the camera on the center of your chest. They typically come in two sizes, which are fairly adjustable.

A wrist housing lets you do exactly what you'd think: You can change the angle whichever way you point your wrist, like a watch.

But sometimes a tiny detail can really matter, and that's when you'll curse your phone's grainy little camera—or simply wish you had more control over a shot. A point and shoot camera dedicated to the task, with an app for sharing on the spot, might be your new best friend.

Many new cameras come with onboard Wi-Fi. It's not like regular Wi-Fi, meaning it can't get you online. This Wi-Fi connection is just for devices to connect to your camera. It will have its own password, so it's not "open." It isn't something you can secure completely when you're using it in public, but it's not like using your computer in Joe's Café—your camera's Wi-Fi use is a very low-risk activity.

Some manufacturers of point and shoot cameras, like Sony, provide you with an app that connects your camera to your phone. This is great for taking better, more detailed photos and getting them online when you're on the scene. When you take both the camera and your phone out to events, you can transfer individual photos to your phone for quick sharing. The app saves it to a folder on your phone, and you can just post it online like normal.

It can help with identifying details, and also acts as an online backup of sorts if you lose your camera or phone. So if you capture something detailed like a lot of faces, uniforms or signs, and it needs to be posted right away, you can.

Make a tiny wearable time-lapse camera

For some, a body camera is a cool idea ... but feels like overkill in practice. Spending hours wearing a little box on your head or strapped in the middle of your chest on a harness isn't everyone's cup of tea. If your idea of hands-free documenting is more subtle and you really prefer less maintenance with your gadgets, consider making a DIY Time Lapse Camera.

This project puts a tiny little camera on a necklace (or clipped to a pocket or strap) where it hangs out and snaps a photo every few seconds for up to two hours. The photos are saved to an SD card (or mini SD), just like in a regular digital camera. Keep it running longer with a portable battery, and bring extra SD cards if you decide to have it quietly snapping pics all day. Transfer the photos into your computer at the end of the day, where you can review or make them into a time lapse video with a program like iMovie.

There are a two great versions of this project; the "DIY Mini Portable Timelapse Camera" uses a mini spy camera, and the "Raspberry Pi Time Lapse Camera" is built using a Raspberry Pi. Find links for both, plus tutorial videos, in the "Digital Revolutionary Project Guide" chapter.

Batteries and cards

There's nothing worse than running out of battery or storage space when you need it most. And someday, you will. Especially if you take your phone out into crowded places, where it will fight for signal and wear the battery down before you know what's happening.

When you pack for an event, always bring extra storage cards for your camera or phone. That way you won't ever have to ration your photo-taking or have to delete anything. You'll also want an extra card or two in case something happens to your camera.

Extra batteries for everything are required in every revolutionary go-bag. It's great that they're cheap and small, and you can find all sizes and shapes on Amazon. Yet you've probably realized by this point that even the nicer portable batteries don't have great lifespans—they die, sometimes far sooner than they should. Then you need a new one, and the cycle begins again.

There's another option, and it has better benefits than the buy-and-dump cycle. Make your own small battery pack for recharging anything that has a USB cord, and you'll be free! My favorite solution is a DIY battery called the MintyBoost, which is easy to put together and has a total cost of around $20. It runs on 2 AA batteries, so you can also boost the environment with rechargeables as you like.

The MintyBoost is a tiny, very powerful USB charger for anything: Your camera, phone, tablet, or anything that needs to be powered-up. The whole thing fits into a little Altoids gum or mint tin. The battery pack will run your gadget for hours, 2.5x more than you'd get from a regular charger.

If you want to get started with hardware hacking or any of the projects in this book, the MintyBoost is the perfect place to start. Find everything you need, including a tutorial on how to solder, in the "Digital Revolutionary Project Guide" chapter at the end of this book.

How to make/use a Wi-Fi "library" of resources, rights, maps

One of the problems we face is access to information. We're kept in the dark about our rights, we're constantly hacking our way through censorship, and everything we use for sharing seems to have a catch. With a tiny bit of tech, and a little easy-to-learn hacking, one solution is to make your own Digital Free Library. With this little gadget, you can stock it with digital documents and anyone around you can connect, download, and share. Put resources like the ACLU's "Know Your Rights" or an area map for a protest march on it, and you might really help someone when they need it.

A Digital Free Library is an electronic Wi-Fi "library" whose concept is similar to something called The Little Free Library. You've probably seen one of these informal community libraries of used books in a café or hotel lobby. It's when a public space has a box or bookshelf where people can take a book, add books, or return books for the community to enjoy. The digital version was originally created to share digital magazines and projects with a neighborhood.

All it takes to make one is a Raspberry Pi Zero, and a Wi-Fi adapter to make a hotspot that people can connect to. Follow this tutorial to make it happen: learn.adafruit.com/digital-free-library/what-youll-need. Consult the next section for more ideas of what to stock in your mobile community library, and find all resource links in the chapter "Digital Revolutionary Project Guide."

Docs to keep with you

In general, it's a good idea to make sure you have your emergency contacts handy. This means your personal emergency contact, but also contact information for a legal hotline, or your lawyer if you have one.

You may want to keep a copy of these somewhere that's not your phone in case something happens to it. Sometimes the best way is the old fashioned way; while some might tell you to put this info on a USB stick, a print copy somewhere on your person is the most practical solution. A post-it stuck to your ID, or even written on your arm in ink (if you think things will be intense) works just fine.

Unless you're aiming for trouble, you should always keep your ID on you. This, and any information about medical conditions and allergies. If you're meeting with people in an unfamiliar building or area, consider keeping a copy of a map or building plan on you as well. Your mapping app might not always be available or fast enough, so either download a copy to your phone or print it to stash in your bag.

Along with these, you may want to consider keeping a few other documents on you that can come in handy if you're confronted by misbehaving authority figures.

On the ACLU's Know Your Rights page (aclu.org/know-your-rights), you'll find a variety of docs that list your rights in different situations. These are great because it's hard to focus when you're under stress. Examples of things you may want to keep with you include "Rights at Airports," "Visits from ICE," "Demonstrations and Protests," "If You're Stopped by Police," "Photographers," "LGBT High School Students," and more.

Other popular documents to carry include the Bill of Rights, the U.S. Constitution, and the EFF's Know Your Rights.

Make an open source protest sign

One of the best parts of being a digital revolutionary is making a better version of something, and then using it. Take the ordinary protest sign. It has one message, and pretty much just one function: That message. What if you had a sign you could change while you're in the moment? And it glowed in the dark?

That's the Open Source Protest Sign, and it's a snap to build. With a little bit of basic hardware hacking, the only thing standing between you and the most amazing sign you can imagine is an hour of your time and ideas about what to say. The Open Source Protest Sign is a wireless project, where one side will be glowing LED lights you command, and the other can be a whiteboard.

Simply make what's called a Raspberry Pi Zero wireless sign, by following the tutorial at Adafruit (links are in the "Digital Revolutionary Project Guide" chapter). The device can also be made into a stand-alone wireless broadcaster with a library of documents, like the Wi-Fi library described in the previous section. Make an expanded version by incorporating an Adafruit FONA that can call your lawyer if the sign is taken away or damaged, or message your friends if it looks like there's trouble ahead.

Security gadgets: YubiKey

When it comes to logging in, you should use 2-step verification (sometimes called 2FA) with every service that'll let you. You can strengthen (and simplify) this by using a secure USB key. It's an actual, physical key that can go on your keychain, and you just plug it into whichever device you're using to sign in. They're inexpensive, and easy to use.

USB keys are gaining in popularity, and Google and Facebook have added this functionality to their log-in processes. It's for people who don't mind carrying a key around with them, and comes with the bonus that you can still securely log in when there's no Wi-Fi or cellular data available. One popular, reputable brand is called YubiKey. Some hackers always carry a YubiKey with them everywhere they go.

The key is used instead of having a code texted to your phone or sent via email (both of which have their disadvantages, like if you lose your phone). It means you need to have the key on you in order to get into your Google or Facebook accounts. You're a lot harder to hack if you use a USB key, and it's also that much harder for nosy, overstepping authorities to access your accounts should your phone get confiscated.

Phishing, malware and other attack methods simply won't work because they'd need your username and password, and to plug in your YubiKey to work. The little USB key acts like two-factor authentication for any service or site you register it with (ones that support two-factor, that is). What's more, it requires no special software, works across multiple devices, and rides along discreetly on your keychain. You can find them online at Amazon and other shopping spots.

Security gadgets: PortaPow

Attacks like ransomware, viruses, and trojans can spread between devices when you connect them, but often times we can only charge our phones or tablets from a USB port. This means we run the risk of viruses or data hacking if we pull a little extra battery life from an unknown socket. Plus, it usually means slow charging. PortaPow solves all of these problems: it's a lightning-fast charge and blocks the transfer of data. PortaPow's Micro USB Cable is the same thing but in micro cord form: it prevents your device going into data transfer mode by blocking data on the line, and like the PortaPow USB, it charges faster than standard USB cables. This is another one you'll find easily on Amazon.

Security gadgets: RFID wallet

If you've been keeping up with the news, you may know that malicious hackers can easily clone your passport or steal your credit card, debit, or driver's license credentials just by brushing up against your wallet or purse. That's because anything with an RFID (Radio-Frequency Identification) chip in it can be cloned by someone using very inexpensive hacking tools.

The only way to prevent that is to carry an RFID-blocking wallet or passport case, which physically blocks this kind of personal breach. They can be found on Fossil, Amazon, and Tumi, among others.

Security gadgets: Emergency lock picks

Picking locks isn't hard to learn, but few people pick up the skill. If you ever get locked out of your house, need to get out of handcuffs, or don't want to call some creepy locksmith to help you get into your home, then you should learn how to use a set of lock picks. Learning to pick locks isn't illegal (unless you're in Japan), and it's great for learning how secure—or not—a lock is. You can find a lot of great tutorials on YouTube.

A small set of lock picks will fit into a bag no problem, but you can find very small sets that pin to a lapel, or slide unnoticeably into a wallet. The Lock-Pick Card is a wallet-sized card that's actually a nine-piece lock pick toolkit. Simply snap the tools out of the card whenever you need to save your own bacon.

Security gadgets: Onion Pi

One of the most popular "snake oil" privacy gadgets is the so-called "Tor in a box." This is (supposedly) a plug-and-play gadget that promises to make you anonymous online by running Tor—a browser people use for anonymity—in a separate gadget. The thing that "anonymity box" fakers don't want you to know is that it's cheap to securely make your own "Tor in a box." It's called an Onion Pi, and it actually works.

Tor is great for privacy and anonymous browsing, but it's not a "silver bullet" solution for being perfectly anonymous. Read about its pluses, minuses, and quirks before you use it. These are detailed in Chapter 5, "Defy Surveillance."

Not everyone who wants to browse anonymously can install Tor on their device, laptop, or work computer. Plus, some devices don't have Ethernet ports. The Onion Pi solves both of these quandaries. The Onion Pi is also a great solution for guests or friends who want to use Tor but doesn't have the ability or time to run Tor on their computer.

The Onion Pi is an excellent gadget for dedicated privacy and security enthusiasts. It lets you browse the internet anonymously anywhere you go with its Onion Pi Tor proxy. This weekend project isn't for beginners, though Adafruit's tutorial practically does most of the work for you. You'll need hardware hacking and programming skills. If you go with Adafruit for the project, you can get all the parts in one kit for $69.95. The end result is a small, portable, low-power privacy gateway for all your internetting, and uses a Raspberry Pi, a USB Wi-Fi adapter, and Ethernet cable.

Follow the Onion Pi tutorials, including the "Raspberry Pi as Wi-Fi Access Point" tutorial at Adafruit (all links are in the "Digital Revolutionary Project Guide" chapter). They explain how to set it up and install Tor. with helpful scripting, code, and tests to run.

The final result is easy to use. Plug the Ethernet cable in anywhere you'd like to access the Internet. Give it power: Plug the Onion Pi into your laptop or a wall adapter with its micro USB cable. Your little Pi will come alive, showing up in your Wi-Fi list as a secure wireless access point called Onion Pi. Connect to it, and you're using Tor—automatically routing your web browsing through the anonymizing Tor network.

Charlatans and bad activist advice

A magic anonymity and privacy box that makes all internetting safe for activists and those who want to avoid surveillance? Apps with "military grade encryption" that promise a "cloak of invisibility" and protects against ransomware? More like a pack of dangerous lies. Alarmingly, these lies are told specifically to activists and people who are at risk of being targeted for surveillance.

Combined with heightened public concern about hacking and security, a never-ending wave of too-good-to-be-true privacy gadgets and apps have been steadily hitting the market and putting people at risk with their false claims of security and enhanced privacy. It's a problem that isn't going away anytime soon.

The security snake oil salesman is one of the most disturbing trends to come out of all the constant government-surveillance headlines. With a new administration putting government trust at an all-time low and our interest in security and privacy at an all-time high, these profiteers are swindling unknowing users with fake gadgets like crazy.

Despite debunkings, these "magic privacy box" charlatans keep coming. Because there's a lack of awareness, people keep funding them on sites like Kickstarter, and crowdfunding sites don't seem well-equipped (or interested enough) to stop them. On top if it all, the security reporting gold rush has produced a green crop of security reporters who, for now at least, are easily fooled into believing these entrepreneurs' claims and unintentionally send trusting consumers off to buy these awful, risky products.

Real security products that do what they promise, especially gadgets, are few and far between. Just because they get a glowing write-up in a mainstream news outlet, it doesn't mean they're on the level.

Look for red flags when you shop, and keep an eye out for trouble. There is no such thing as "military grade encryption," which has been a claim that's only recently started to get debunked. Other claims, such as "protects from crypto-lockers" or "would have prevented the Sony hack" are flat-out false. Same goes for lies like "No more backdoors!" and "leaves no trace on your computer," as well as claims saying "it can be used inside countries like North Korea safely."

If the people behind the product act weird, something's wrong. When people asked technical questions about a "Tor in a box" gadget on Kickstarter called Anonabox, the inventor went on the attack, avoided the questions, used a barrage of buzzwords, and played mind games. Security snake oil product Sever's founder made a bizarre video to mock the highly respected InfoSec professionals who asked questions and wrote criticism.

Do they claim to make the whole thing from scratch, or suggest a fishy history of prototypes? Something's rotten, and you should stay away.

If a product promises a "powerful new" or "secret" encryption algorithm, something's not right. Same if it describes basic Internet or computer functions as if they are special features, or claims to be open source and proprietary at the same time. As a general rule, run far and fast from anything that confuses (or conflates) privacy and anonymity, promises super speeds, or is a privacy product that comes with an app store.

Use the power of search. Google for blog posts, where researchers might have debunked crazy claims, and definitely search Twitter, where InfoSec communities will chat about the gadgets and pick them apart. Search by using the product's name as a hashtag.

Security gadgets are one instance where you actually should read the comments. Few people understand security minutiae, let alone the basics in ways security pros do—so it remains all too easy for fakers to hype the hacking fears, make impossible promises, take the money, and run.

Security professionals are very interested in these gadgets, and they hate these charlatans. You'll often find the comments on a Kickstarter brimming with questions and answers... And they're not shy about pointing out when something is fishy, or false. Case in point is the site securitysnakeoil.org, where the author does individual analysis on crowdfunded security products, and documents each bogus product's bizarre lifecycle. Their Twitter account @secsnakeoil is where you'll see commentary on a wider range of products and more frequent news items.

Also essential for research is attrition.org/errata that "exists to enlighten readers about errors, omissions, incidents, lies and charlatans in the security industry." This is where you'll find news about companies that ship malware with their products, security software "that may do more harm than good," bio pages on actual charlatans in the security industry, and more.

The same problems are happening with online advice for anonymity, surveillance, and other pressing privacy and security issues. Bad activist advice is rampant. When you see Medium or other posts about defeating facial recognition surveillance, being totally anonymous online, or securing your phone for crossing a border, proceed with extreme caution. Most of us know that you should always double-check and research what we read online. But that's doubly important when it comes to learning about things that are supposed to protect you from being hacked, surveilled, or exposed to harm online.

But it's tough to tell the good advice from the bad when it comes to privacy, security, identity protection, and things like surveillance. These topics come with complicated technical aspects that not a lot of people know or understand. Which makes it a ripe arena for exploitation by people who mean harm, or just want to look like they're "experts." Especially in an area as trendy online as digital activism. And the trendy anti-surveillance crowd tend to be people who haven't endured a genuine risk in their lives, with little inclination to empathy for people who can't afford iPhones.

   If something doesn't look right, or you can't find anyone to answer your questions about it, then avoid it. Use your bullshit detector. The advice to read the comments and see what security professionals are saying (on social media and blogs) applies here just as strongly as with shopping for security gadgets. People who work in InfoSec and in the trenches of fighting for online privacy have more than a work-related stake in making sure accurate information is out there. It's personal for them.

CHAPTER 7

FIGHT CENSORSHIP

The control and suppression of opinions, ideas, words, images, and information is the hallmark of oppression. Whether it's done by a despotic government regime, a company, an algorithm, or an individual, it's censorship. This is the imposing of political or moral values on others, and it comes in different forms.

They ways you'll encounter censorship will vary. Considering how conservative and easily-abused social networks are, you've probably already dealt with censorship in one way or another already.

This is especially true if you speak up about controversial topics, or have anything to do with human sexuality in life or art. You might be censored by a social network for posting a photo or video, or even for criticizing the network itself. It's possible that your meme, posts, or other media gets censored by other people, who attempt to silence you by unfairly reporting your post or account for Terms of Service violations.

Or, you've encountered censorship when you've tried to access controversial or non-conservative information online—from content filters. Like when a government pressures an Internet provider to filter or shut off access to users.

When you're censored online, no one can find you—and you can't tell anyone you're being silenced. Censorship happens in secret. This chapter shines a light on what's going on with online censorship and how it directly affects you—and gives you tools to fight with.

How they censor you

The Open Net Initiative (opennet.net) identifies four different kinds of Internet censorship: Technical methods, search request removals, takedowns, and induced self-censorship.

Technical methods include IP blocking, DNS tampering, and URL blocking using a proxy. According to Open Net, these techniques block specific pages, URLs, or IP addresses. "These methods are most frequently used where direct jurisdiction or control over websites are beyond the reach of authorities," they explain. Further, "keyword blocking, which blocks access to websites based on the words found in URLs or blocks searches involving blacklisted terms, is a more advanced technique that a growing number of countries are employing."

Search request removals are exactly what it sounds like. A government asks or pressures a search company like Google to exclude websites and terms from search results.

This can also be done in developer circles with a search that's done in apps and on specific sites, for reasons either moral, political or personal. In 2015, someone found my name in a list of banned search terms that was used as the basis for a large commercial photo website. The list had been copied and used in hundreds of other projects. It took considerable work to fix the issue, and the originator of the "banned words" list ignored everyone's requests for an explanation. Most people assumed his ambivalence to these inquiries indicated that he disliked me or my work. The end result in any situation with banned, blocked, or removed search terms is that the topic, term, and websites can't be found. The person or the thing is simply erased.

Takedown censorship is when an entity legally demands the removal of websites. Open Net explains that in many countries, "a cease and desist notice sent from one private party to another, with the threat of subsequent legal action, is enough to convince web hosts to take down websites ... Where authorities have control of domain name servers, officials can deregister a domain that is hosting restricted content, making the website invisible to the browsers of users seeking to access the site."

Induced self-censorship is something we've seen a lot of with the various election propaganda wars on social media, and with harassment and bullying of people in movements such as Black Lives Matter. People are pressured to self-censor both in browsing habits, for fear of surveillance, and in choosing what they do (or don't) post online. Self-censorship is an enormous tool leveraged on social networks, whose methods of preventing abuse (and its resulting intimidation and silencing) are all quite broken. Additionally, ONI tells us "the threat of legal action, the promotion of social norms, or informal methods of intimidation" are also used to censor our voices online.

Finally, there's algorithmic censorship. Keyword censoring largely fuels this, yet some social networks have been taking it a step further. Facebook scans and tracks the private messages and posts of its users, censoring out content at its discretion (and without explanation or recourse).

Many LGBT users of the site who have written posts asking about being targeted for "real names" or alleged content infractions have reported having these messages and posts deleted. In the case of a public post takedown where a drag queen was inquiring if her friends were having the same issues, she immediately got an automated message saying post violated "safety" rules on the site. Censorship is now automated, for the safety of corporate interests.

When governments censor

Governments, Internet service providers, Wi-Fi apps, airline Wi-Fi, and public networks all censor web content from users. Most people don't know it's happening. It can starve legitimate businesses from traffic and revenue, and keep people from learning about democracy or life outside their country. It can prevent the public from finding out about state-sanctioned violence, and oppress ideas by "disappearing" art, film, writing, or people. It can make online work impossible in airplanes or at cafes, or prevent someone from finding a resource they desperately need.

A government might force providers to keep websites and news topics from its citizens—or a government might force an Internet blackout on its citizens during times of protest. So-called "family friendly" filters used by public Wi-Fi providers and companies like Open DNS seek to prevent access to pornography, gambling, and hate speech. But they always get it wrong, and their automation invariably prevents people from accessing things like breast cancer sites, LGBT news, and violence prevention resources.

When we talk about Internet censorship, most people think of what's called the "Great Firewall of China." This refers to laws and technologies implemented by the Chinese government to closely monitor the activity of Internet users within the country, and block access to information and websites the government doesn't like. If you're curious, the site greatfirewallofchina.org can tell you if a website is blocked or not.

For instance, people in China searching for Amnesty International won't be able to find or access anything about the organization. *The New York Times* was blocked in China until 2001; an article the Chinese government didn't like got the *Times* re-blocked in 2012. In March 2017 the *Times* wrote, "Our Android app was never accepted in Chinese Android stores and recently Apple removed our iOS app from their Chinese app store, most certainly because of Chinese government pressure." The paper's censorship in China is aided by Apple and Android stores, who bend to the will of the government.

In 2011, all traffic from the country of Syria to the rest of the Internet simply stopped. The Syrian Minister of Information told press that the government did not "turn off" the Internet, but the U.S. State Department believed otherwise. Syria shut down its Internet just in time for the largest anti-government protest of the country's uprising. While the Internet was off, terrible things happened. During the blackout, Syrian authorities opened fire into crowds of protesters, killing over 72 people, while government forces assaulted towns seen as key to the demonstrations, killing even more. It wasn't the only time.

Other Internet censorship feels softer, but it's no less insidious. In the UK, government-driven filters are implemented at the ISP level. Internet customers in the UK have their Internet access filtered "by default," meaning that users have to "opt out" if they want an unfiltered Internet experience. The filtering program began in 2013, after the government basically strong-armed ISP's into complying under the guise of protecting children from online pornography—a frequent line from censors.

The UK's filtering program has been so uneven and defiantly untransparent that it has censored a wide range of websites. The "Great British Firewall's" website overblocking has included sex education, suicide prevention, drug advice, child protection services, rape and domestic violence services, and more. The Open Rights Group became so frustrated and appalled, they created blocked.org.uk so people can find out whether or not their site is being blocked.

Filters, shutdowns, and company collusion with governments all happen behind closed doors. Their targets, reasoning, and lists are never disclosed, and any excuses given to press can seldom be trusted. Amnesty International, the ACLU, and Human Rights Watch all monitor Internet censorship and have calls to action worth keeping an eye on. The Open Net Initiative has complete documentation and an index on global Internet filtering, as well as interactive maps.

Circumvention tools

While you'd need advanced technical help in a country where the Internet has been shut off, getting around blocks and filters in most locations can be done with a few simple circumvention tools. The primary ways to get around filters and Internet censorship are with the same things most recommended to protect against hacking and surveillance: Tor ("The Onion Router") and VPNs (Virtual Private Networks).

Avoid censorship:

- Turn off "quality filters" on social media accounts
- Turn off "safe search"
- Use a VPN, Tor or Tails (blocks and blacklists)

There are a few ways to bypass the technical aspects of Internet censorship, namely web blocks and filtering. In general, techniques include cached (copied and saved) web pages, website mirrors and archives (duplicates of websites on different URLs), alternate DNS servers, SSH tunneling, proxy websites, virtual private networks (VPNs), and other circumvention software tools like Tor or the Tails operating system.

RSS aggregators like Feedly can let you receive RSS feeds that might be on sites that are blocked directly. Half of those techniques require having access to the unfiltered Internet in the first place. For most people, a VPN is the answer.

Why is everyone saying I should use Tor?

Countries that tightly censor their Internet also surveil it, and monitor traffic for threats to their censorship. This can include looking for unusual activity, and the installation of popular circumvention tools like Tor ("The Onion Router"). This is unfortunate, because helping at-risk people circumvent filters and surveillance is exactly what Tor was made for. Read more about installing and using Tor to fight spying (and what Tor does and *doesn't* do for you) in Chapter 5, "Defy Surveillance."

Tor is an oft-recommended tool for dissidents and whistleblowers that want to avoid censorship or being tracked online. The Tor Project is the nonprofit organization behind the software. Its culture is one of anti-surveillance activists with strong beliefs and the rabid fans (and detractors) that come with it. Its proponents like to recommend it as an all-purpose anti-surveillance, anti-censorship remedy.

This is pretty problematic. The software has its limitations and has gone for significant amounts of time in the past with security holes in it—ones that have been exploited by the U.S. government. While it is true that Tor can be used with the legitimate goal of anonymity on the Internet, it is also used for accessing sites on the 'darknet' or 'dark web' the underground network of .onion websites that aren't exposed to the wider Internet. So, naturally, Tor is of enormous interest to law enforcement, and government hackers spend a lot of effort figuring out ways to break it.

Tor is also a well-known circumvention tool that can make you look suspicious if authorities are watching for such activity. So if you're in a heated situation and suddenly start using Tor (or any form of encrypted communications), you will draw the unwanted attention of the authorities, which is of particular concern to activists. You are using a new technology, and this will make you stand out, which can raise flags and potentially see you subjected to closer surveillance. Some places ban the use of Tor on their network or Wi-Fi. Setting up a Tor node inside a network runs a risk of an organization's IP being added to an Internet blacklist, notably if the node is involved in suspicious activities.

Tor is great for some things. Generally, it is excellent for covering your tracks. Tor routes your Internet traffic through what's called an overlay network, which makes it difficult for nosy people to follow the path your data takes and trace it back to you. Along the way multiple layers of encryption are used to hide your true IP address, thus the onion metaphor. Another option is the Tails operating system, which you should read more about in Chapter 5, "Defy Surveillance."

Unfortunately, Tor is not always great for getting around blocks and filters, because you may not be able to access some websites. Most services that protect websites from DDoS will stop Tor users from accessing the site. (A Distributed Denial of Service is an attack that overloads a site with traffic, and Tor is often used in the attack.) In addition, Tor's default security settings will break some websites or make them unusable altogether by blocking scripts and other features. Unless you really know what you're doing, changing these settings can affect your privacy.

A VPN is a better choice for many people in most situations. There's no need to resort to Tor to bypass web filtering unless there's a real risk of being dragged away in the middle of the night due to your web browsing habits.

Everyone should have a VPN
Connecting to a VPN (Virtual Private Network) server that's outside your own country will also let you bypass censorship. These services and apps make it incredibly easy with their simple interfaces. Plus, a VPN is a lot less conspicuous. You're more likely

to blend in by using a VPN because they're everywhere, marketed to regular people who want to be safe from hacking. According to GlobalWebIndex, over 400 million people use virtual private networks to circumvent censorship or for an increased level of privacy. You should always use one when you travel, regardless any censorship concerns, for your own safety.

Where Tor bounces your traffic through a bunch of servers to make your IP random, with a VPN you pick a server in the country you want your traffic to look like it's coming from. Most VPN services have around a dozen countries you can choose from at any time, and all the reputable ones have mobile and tablet versions, too.

It's important to choose a safe a reputable VPN. Flip over to Chapter 5, "Defy Surveillance," to read in detail everything you need to know about selecting and using a VPN.

Social network censorship

No one censors its users better than Facebook. The social media monopoly takes down videos, photos, posts, accounts, pages, and even your private messages if it doesn't like them. It has removed one of the world's most important war photos, images of culturally essential (and classical) artwork, and videos of human rights abuses. It has allowed videos of child abuse, rapes, and murders stay online. Its censorship is harmful to society, and there is no doubt that it has helped erode our free speech and capacity for empathy—for this is what art and free speech does, along with keep us free as a society.

We can't trust the company's excuses or explanations, nor can we guess as to why this is. The company offers no proof or verification of its claims when evading accountability. We can only judge its actions in censorship, which aid conservatism and repressive regimes, and fly in the face of art and free expression as values intrinsic to human rights.

Keep this in mind when you upload and share anything to Facebook. It doesn't care about following its own rules, for it makes exceptions for celebrities, politicians, and governments all the time. It doesn't care about you, or the social importance of your media— unless the press makes a stink about it. Luckily for Facebook, few people have access to this kind of leverage. Facebook is a tool for distribution but it cannot be trusted with anything important. It's the lowest bar, and it gives you an example of what to expect when you're dealing with the worst practices in fairness and censorship.

Like Facebook, Twitter facilitates censorship by those who maliciously use reporting tools. This has been an issue since the Internet's beginning: The "report abuse" function has been used on almost every social media site to silence and censor other users. It's a problem you'd think would be solved by now, but in my opinion it's an issue that won't be until we get more decision makers behind the scenes who from groups likely to be silenced by such censorship. As in, not the people who are currently making and running our social networks.

Companies are beyond terrible at protecting their users from this; it is literally not a real concern for them. That's because the people at these companies can't imagine it happening to them. And for us, it feels incredibly personal.

Google censors too, and so does Instagram (they're as bad as their parent company, Facebook). YouTube has similar issues with abuse of their reporting systems, and they only recently stopped censoring LGBT videos as "adult content."

Fight censorship:

- Make copies of everything
- Document attackers
- Document your censorship ordeal (screencaps)
- Know the site's redress policy
- Find others with the same experience
- Find others not being censored
- Share everything with followers and press

Unfortunately for us, this censorship is both part of the problem and a fact of life. When you speak up about injustice, people will try to report you for anything they can. You will be censored, and unfairly. To expect it is to be prepared. Always make backup copies of everything, and screencap anything you think might get taken down.

When this happens to you, make noise. Lots of it.

How to use SecureDrop

There may come a time when you want to share or send something to a journalist or news outlet securely and anonymously. Or, you may face censorship so egregious that you are compelled to share your message or information with the press. These are high-risk situations. That's when you'll see if the media outlet you'd like to share it with has SecureDrop on their website.

SecureDrop is an open-source software platform created to facilitate secure communication between journalists and their sources (or whistleblowers). It was originally conceived and built under the name DeadDrop by hackers Aaron Swartz and Kevin Poulsen.

SecureDrop has been widely adopted by press and various organizations around the world. Outlets like T*he Washington Post, The Guardian, The New Yorker, The New York Times, Buzzfeed, The Intercept,* and *ProPublica* (among others) each have a Secure Drop available through their regular websites.

Using it is done in steps. SecureDrop uses Tor, and each media outlet's SecureDrop website is only accessible on the Tor network.

Download and install the Tor browser. Take your security a step further and install the Tails operating system to use while you engage with SecureDrop. Tails has a great setup assistant on its website that walks you through the installation process (tails.boum.org/install/index.en.html). Tor and the Tails operating system have their limits, so be sure read up about them Chapter 5. Make sure you're accessing the Internet safely; don't use your home or work network. *The Guardian* recommends:

> "You should avoid using the platform on small networks where Tor usage may be monitored or restricted, or in public places where your screen may be viewed by CCTV. We recommend that you don't jump straight from this landing page to the SecureDrop site when uploading, especially on business networks that may be monitored. Best practice would be to

make a note of the Tor url and upload your content from a different machine at a later time."

Then copy and paste the unique Tor address provided by your media outlet of choice into the address bar. When the page loads, you will find specific instructions on how to submit files and messages to the outlet.

After this, you'll be assigned a random "code name." If a reporter or editor from the press outlet wants to contact you, they'll do so in the SecureDrop platform. Those messages are the only way they'll contact you, so don't lose or forget your code name.

Getting our messages out and having access to information is becoming critical for our survival. The fight against censorship in all its forms may feel like an uphill battle, but the more of us who know how to fight it, the better we can beat it back into the Dark Ages where it belongs.

CHAPTER 8

THE REVOLUTION WILL BE SHARED

In his 2007 TED Talk, war photographer James Nachtwey explained that he grew up in a time when war was raging in Vietnam. Politicians were telling the American public one thing, while photographers were showing something completely different. "Their images fueled resistance to the war and to racism," he said. "They not only recorded history; they helped change the course of history." Nachtwey explained that "their pictures became part of our collective consciousness and, as consciousness evolved into a shared sense of conscience, change became not only possible, but inevitable."

Cameras can't be denied. They are objective observers, and they provide expert testimony. Bearing witness—the act of witnessing and sharing it with others—ensures that our stories are heard and transcend time. It is also vital for healing from trauma.

Sharing online allows us to be catalysts for change. With our documentation and sharing we can create sympathy and raise awareness, or offer critical commentary. And as Nachtwey pointed out a decade ago, we can show that "what happens at ground level, far from the halls of power, happens to ordinary citizens one by one."

Make sure your media is seen

The last thing you want is your post or share getting buried in a timeline before your followers can see it, and you want them to go as wide as possible. There are a lot of little things that'll help you accomplish both of these things, and they don't even involve trickery. Much.

Unless it's a Medium essay or blog post with detailed information, make your tweets and posts short and easy to understand. If you're sharing a link, give it a simple and intriguing one-sentence description. Your line could be a great short quote from the article, or saying something personal, like that it really opened your eyes. Use words that trigger action like "how," "what," and "why." Make unique media: For instance, a handy portable mini-projector (like Artlii, which connects to an iPhone) and images that convey a message can create great photo and video opportunities.

Always append a hashtag. This makes sure your post is included in a much larger conversation, and gets collected in social media monitoring tools following the topic. And algorithms like it—making your search result more favorable. Research your hashtags to make sure no one's saying anything with them that might cause a problem for you.

Photos and videos will make algorithms favor your posts, too. They'll be more likely to surface in searches and on people's timelines that are "curated" by the website. That's because social media sites want to encourage (read: reward) users that "engage" more than those who don't.

Share important things four times (and be creative about it). Don't spam your followers—that's like committing social media suicide. Yet if you share something once on Twitter, you'll get the most response the first time. The second time will get you far less engagement. But the second and third times might add up to twice as much as just sharing it once. And that's worth it. You can do more, but be careful to not annoy your followers. Share it once, then again the same day. Once again the following day. Again in one week.

Engage with other users. Ask questions, re-share their comments, and retweet their comments about you (or the topic). This adds up to more visibility in other people's timelines and mentions. Another thing that helps with being seen is paying attention to what time it is in your time zone, and others. Post when people are awake and active.

Make sure you have a place to send people. Don't talk about anything (especially events or groups) unless you have a real link to share. That link can be a blog post with more information, a website, or anything where people will get their questions answered. Don't make Facebook or Instagram your only link for interested outsiders, or in place of an actual website for your group, because Facebook is most likely to censor, delete, or restrict you for no reason.

How to use live video

Facebook, Instagram, Twitter (Periscope), and YouTube are the primary livestreaming creation and social sharing sites as of this writing. Each of them has different instructions for sharing live video.

YouTube is where to broadcast live video that you actually want to save and have people find. Livestreaming from the YouTube app is simple; click the big red capture button in the corner, take or choose a thumbnail photo, and you're streaming. Your YouTube subscribers are all alerted that you're streaming, and you can enable a chat function if you want to talk to viewers as you're streaming. The recording is archived when you're done, and the video is searchable by anyone. YouTube has no time restrictions for live broadcasts, so you can "go live" as long as you want.

To livestream on Twitter's Periscope, you need to be using the Twitter app. To livestream, you'll compose a Tweet then tap "LIVE." Next you'll be on a pre-broadcast screen so you can frame your shot. Then press "Go Live" to start broadcasting. Anyone on the Twitter mobile app can see it and comment on it. There is no time limit for live video on Twitter; some people even do "sleep casts." You can save the video (without comments) to your phone camera roll if you want to keep it.

Facebook streaming begins when you click the little "Live" icon and give the app access to your camera and microphone. Click "continue" and choose your privacy setting. Next, write a short and compelling description. Before you click "Go Live," check your camera's view. If you want to change to front or back camera, click the little rotating arrow icon. When you click "Go Live" you'll get a countdown before it starts streaming. Your video appears in your News Feed (and some people's News Feeds, subject to its algorithm) like any other post. Facebook lets you stream for up to 90 minutes.

With Instagram Live you get no replays, and the video "disappears" after it's done. To livestream on Instagram, tap on the "Your Story" profile photo (with the + sign next to it). This takes you to your Instagram Stories, where you pick one of three options. "Live" is shooting a video that disappears after the broadcast ends.

"Normal" has the video disappearing in 24 hours. "Boomerang" is a time-lapse-like video created from a burst of photos, and is not a livestream. Check all your Instagram Story settings before you click "Start Live Video." The time limit for live broadcasts is one hour.

Livestreaming concerns

Livestreaming from a phone, wither it's with YouTube, Periscope, or any other app, brings people to the front lines. Showing the march, protest or revolution as it's happening is a powerful tool for awareness and change. It also kills misinformation and propaganda.

Livestreaming comes with risks, too. Police don't like it, and they may target you if they perceive it as a threat. Sometimes citizens will not want to be in your livestream; in extreme situations livestreamers have been attacked by their fellow protesters. That might be because people in the video face retribution or persecution for participating in what you've filmed.

If things get intense or you witness what may be human rights violations, your urge will be to livestream it.

First, look around you and make sure you're not in immediate danger. In Chapter 9 ("Taking It to the Streets") you will learn about having a spotter; if this person is with you, put them into action so someone is watching out for your safety while you film. If you may get hurt and you see others recording the incident, choose safety over duplicating the work of others. It's best for you to be able to resist another day.

Recording protesters and authorities poses ethical questions for the one doing the filming that you'll want to consider. In countries with oppressive governments, law enforcement will often comb over recordings, photos, and posts after an event in an attempt to identify protesters, who are then targeted for harassment or worse. If this is a potential problem, use an app like Obscuracam that allows you to blur faces.

Your identity is also a consideration. Recording and sharing puts you identifiably at the scene of a protest or event, too.

As a general rule, you should always check to make sure your location (as "metadata" or "EXIF data") is being removed from photos and videos you upload. Every pic and video has its own little file in it that has a bunch of info, like which camera you used and its settings, as well as location data—where and when it was made. Most services let you choose not to have this information included in your file or upload. Look at your settings with each app you use for pics and videos and see if it gives you this option. Then turn it off for safety from trolls and creeps.

If the app or device doesn't let you remove or turn off your location from media you share, or you need to go a step further and wipe all the other potentially identifying information from your media, use a tool to remove the metadata with a tool like CameraV.

Those wishing to anonymize their media entirely or keep identities separate will want to make sure they use a VPN (like Tunnelbear) or Tor (Orbot for mobile) on their devices to do the uploads, too. Look into using apps designed for documenting human rights abuses, like eyeWitness to Atrocities and Mobile Martus.

Keep all of this in mind if you choose to livestream. Consider looking at "best practices" guides from organizations that work toward exposing abuses and protecting victims within the digital media realm. Check out the Witness blog (blog.witness.org), whose post "Video As Evidence: Basic Practices" is extremely helpful for navigating your livestreaming choices.

Create memes that matter

Memes make us laugh, and a steady diet of good ones can keep us sane while we navigate a world that feels like it's out to get our mental health at every turn. They're also incredible rallying points for ideas; creating empathy, communicating ideas, and raising awareness. They proliferate rapidly through the social communities of the Internet, like Twitter, Reddit, Facebook, and others. Sometimes they annoy, but often they provide levity when we really need it.

Love them or hate them, memes now shape the world and us. They spread new information, and create a space where an idea becomes something people rally around. They can turn hateful political movements upside down.

One great example of all of this is the "punch a Nazi" meme, which is actually a tale of two memes.

There were a lot of rude awakenings that came with the 2016 election in the United States, but the most brutal (and for some, shocking) was the rise of the fascist Nazi movement--also called the "alt-right." It had been festering for decades, but everyone from national front groups and racist rednecks to Ku Klux Klan and extreme-right wealthy tech fascists came out of the woodwork and into the public eye, believing that their fringe beliefs had been validated by the election of Donald Trump.

One rallying point they had online was the "Pepe the Frog"

meme. The green frog began as a playful cartoon in 2005 whose signature phrase was "feels good, man." White supremacists on message boards made a concerted effort to "reclaim Pepe" from whom they saw as normal people by proliferating art of the frog as a pro-Trump, pro-Nazi symbol. In those communities, it took off—and so-called normal people both distanced themselves from using Pepe memes anymore while seeing the meme as a symbol of hate. It became such a strong symbol for fascists that Pepe the Frog was designated a hate symbol by the Anti-Defamation League in September 2016, two months before the election.

This meme spread, normalizing the new neo-Nazi platform and its messages. The "alt-right" (Nazi) figurehead Richard Spencer used Pepe the Frog memes specifically to communicate and represent his white supremacist ideologies.

While wearing a Pepe the Frog lapel pin, Spencer was interviewed on video and asked about the symbol. Just as he was about to answer, Spencer was punched in the face, live. The video went viral online and heralded the beginning of many "punch a Nazi" memes. The effect was far larger than the reach of one cartoon frog.

These memes are still rolling, and have included everything from tweets of support from the actor who plays Captain America in Marvel films, to memes about punching Nazis based on films like *Raiders of the Lost Ark* and *Inglourious Basterds*. More celebs chimed in, and it was as funny as it was sharply combating the fascist idolatry. Corporate media couldn't ignore the pushback on the new Nazi movement. The conversations began, asking where our society was now that we're back in the World War II era of taking down Nazis in our midst as an act of patriotism.

Memes are almost always parody. They usually have very short life cycles, unless they universally endure like Kermit the Frog or Grumpy Cat. Memes are made for sharing—and appropriation, as well as parody of the original idea itself. You have to be okay with letting it go free for remixing among the world's creators to get your message out.

Elements of a meme are usually as simple as text and image. A great example is the Kermit meme, which has different versions ranging from "Evil Kermit" to " Kermit Drinking Tea." Each image expresses a feeling that people put their own words to. According to Know Your Meme, "Evil Kermit" is a "captioned image series featuring a screenshot of the Muppet character Kermit the Frog talking with his nemesis Constantine dressed as a Sith Lord from Star Wars, who instructs him to perform various indulgent, lazy, selfish and unethical acts."

There are also video memes, which combine a short video with music. Video memes can be based on a short moment of footage, like a clip of Nazi Richard Spencer getting punched in the face to music. Another version of a video meme would be the "Harlem Shake" trend, where people around the world and from all walks of life filmed themselves dancing to one song in a group setting.

The simplest, funniest memes are usually the most powerful. Image and text is the way to go. Some people recommend starting with an image. You may find it easier to start with your phrase. Take a browse through Know Your Meme or different online free meme generators to see what inspires you.

For instance, a gender equality meme might begin for you with an image of two identical parrots kissing, or a dog and cat snuggling together. The caption might hook onto a timely message you're trying to get out, like "Love Trumps Hate: Equal Snuggles For All." You can also use a popular meme phrase and image, like the "Conspiracy Keanu" meme. Visit a meme generator like Imgflip.com and navigate to the Keanu creation page. You'll see the newest featured versions that people are making, which might inspire you.

Test out your memes before sharing them. Be sure they make sense and that they're funny to someone other than yourself. Use your friends, community, or family as test subjects, or make throwaway accounts on message boards to post with and garner response. Once you have a gem, share it widely—set it free!

Measure your impact

You've probably already started interacting on social media sites like Twitter, SnapChat, Medium, Facebook, Tumblr, Google+, Pinterest, YouTube, and Instagram, depending on the type of content you're sharing and what your community already uses. The next step is figuring out if it's having an impact, and what it means for you.

Making a difference with your sharing, messaging, memes, and media making can mean a variety of different things. And evaluating value to the outside world doesn't come naturally for most people. Sharing things that reflect our values and hope seems even harder to measure in terms of impact, probably because we already believe these acts have merit for their own sake--the public good.

That doesn't mean we don't want to know if what we're doing is making a difference. It's not impossible to gauge, thought there are a lot of moving parts to measure depending on what "making a difference" means to you.

Some kinds of measurement are more like milestones and they're easier to count as impact. Did an article get written about the issue or event? Did a politician, celebrity, or influencer talk about it or share your meme? Did someone file a lawsuit based on information you found? Did someone go to jail, were injustices revealed, were people helped? These are all concrete things, and they're also really validating.

Another way to assess if what you're doing is making a difference is to measure your tweets, comments, shares, views, likes, new followers, and all the other metrics you can find. Before you jump in, think about your goals and what it means for you to feel some success. It may be that all you need is to see something shared a few times, or to watch a follower count steadily increase—this would be one way to measure whether or not you're increasing advocates and fans to your cause.

Your goal could be awareness. You might want to see people's opinions changed in comments or discussions on Twitter. Or, your goal might be accomplished through reach—finding a substantial audience, and multiplying the awareness raised. If you want to measure awareness, then use metrics like volume, reach, exposure, and amplification. How far is your message spreading? Also track what people are saying. How much of the overall conversation around a rival hashtag or meme is about yours?

Think about what you're hoping to see happen with your content—also called "engagement." Your priorities might be getting them to read, share, reply, click, remix, comment on, use your hashtag, or otherwise interact with what you're putting out there. To measure this, look for metrics around retweets, comments, replies, and participants. How many people are participating, how often are they participating, and in what forms are they participating?

Surveying everything casually might be enough to satisfy you. But if you want to get more stringent with measuring your impact, don't drive yourself crazy trying to track everything yourself. Use tools that capture your metrics. If you're not sure which app to use, check out the resources at SocDir (socdir.com), which lists hundreds of social media metrics tools.

Then start looking at your metrics and see if they satisfy. You may see something you've missed; maybe Pinterest is a waste of your time. Cut back on anything that seems like it's soaking up too much of your time and resources. Set goals for yourself. Figure out what you can do better, where to focus your attention more, see what people find most interesting, and make changes where needed.

Tools for tracking topics and events

One of the most important ways to resist the normalization of racism, injustice, corruption, and more, is to be persistent about not letting the subjects drop or fade into the background. One way to do that is to track events and topics so you can stay on top of the latest, and keep sharing the important stuff.

Two of the best places to track wider spheres are Twitter, Google News, and Google Trends. Since Twitter is an open platform it's far more useful for breaking news, gathering information, watching interactions, and following individuals than the closed network that's Facebook (which, by the way, is technically a darknet). Additionally, the world's journalists rely on Twitter; it's where we hang out, and also where we work.

You may want to track events as they're happening, like a protest, election, or court case. Or you might be staying on a long-running topic with constantly developing news, like the Trump-Russia investigation or climate change. Either way, you'll need the right tool for the job so you don't go nuts refreshing a hashtag or combing news and social sites by hand.

Social media and news monitoring tools might be your best friend. There are oodles of them to choose from.

Cyfe is a dashboard that lets you track a ton of hashtags and keywords in one spot. Hootsuite has a huge range of tools for searching across multiple social media sites and monitoring trends. Social Mention is just for digging into trending search terms on Twitter. Tweetdeck can be used for monitoring hashtags, among other things.

Top-Hashtags monitors the tags trending on Instagram. Mention is a paid service starting at $20 a month that offers a comprehensive monitoring system across, well, everything. Anewstip is a search engine for finding journalists, influencers and media outlets that have recently mentioned a topic on Twitter.

There are many more, and new ones are coming out all the time. The majority of social media monitoring tools are for PR and media professionals, a market that's only growing. Their tools for "boosting brands" are perfect for incorporating into your digital arsenal; Google for blog posts about these tools and you'll find long review lists.

Personally, I think these monitoring tools also count as self-care, since they let you automate something that would otherwise add to your stress levels. Plus you'll feel a lot better about putting effort into making and sharing media when you can see it's making an impact.

CHAPTER 9

TAKING IT TO THE STREETS

Our voices are undeniable when they're witnessed, documented, and accessible for all to see online. It's one powerful component of being an agent of change. The other is to show up.

Going to town halls, rallies, marches, events, and public gatherings is how to literally make change happen. People in person cannot be ignored, denied, or have their existence lied about to constituents, press, or those in power. Mass demonstrations and marches have made it impossible for issues to go away, everywhere from Egypt and Paris to Ferguson and San Francisco.

Spontaneous gatherings can bring immediate action. When Trump tried to ban Muslims from traveling into the United States, hundreds of thousands of American citizens dropped everything and went to their nearby airports.

The ban resulted in travelers from certain Muslim countries being detained, as well as holders of green cards and visas, simply because of the country they were traveling from (and, we later found out, because of their appearance). Elderly people, families, and children were held without food or water for hours, and some were ultimately refused entry into the US. Families were torn apart. Those targeted had their civil rights and their privacy violated as border authorities forcibly searched their bodies, their belongings, and their digital devices.

Outside the impromptu detention centers in airports everywhere, there were crowds of people gathering. They came from all walks of life, all backgrounds, all races, professions, genders, and religious. Attorneys sat on the floor in waiting areas pulling together the legal paperwork to help the detainees. Taxi drivers went on strike. Crowds held signs opposing this discriminatory presidential order motivated by racism and religious prejudice.. Protesters demanded release of the innocent travelers, and an immediate stop to the detentions and other forms of anti-immigrant and anti-Muslim discrimination. They filmed, photographed, documented and instantly shared what was happening, as it happened.

And it worked. Their presence brought global press attention, and forces lawmakers and authorities into the limelight of public scrutiny. The victims not only had advocates putting their real human faces and names into the spotlight, but it created a crisis that lawmakers and authorities could not evade. The crowds overflowed, and refused to leave until every last detained person was released.

If you want justice, you have to show up. But not everyone can drop their lives and rush to the airport. We can still participate when we can't do so in person. Thanks to our connected world, there are plenty of ways you can "show up" without being there. This chapter is all about how to show up and make the opposition feel your presence, no matter if you're there with feet on the ground or amplifying the street-level message from afar.

Digital safety in public

Going to any political event, whether organized or spontaneous, means you're going to be under surveillance. That means you might get your picture taken and shared online by others, you might end up on a video that goes viral or gets on CNN, and you will certainly be under some sort of phone surveillance. At this time, there is no reliable way to avoid the facial recognition software that's used on public security cameras and other recording devices, unless you cover your face with a mask or bandana.

Up to this point, everything you've read in this book has prepared you to minimize (or remove) your surveillance footprint, and to make your devices better at protecting your privacy. Your main concerns when doing in-person protest will be having your cell service intercepted by "stingrays" (IMEI/IMSI, described in Chapter 5), or having your phone confiscated, or even being compelled to unlock your phone by authorities. Remember: Your phone can be used to track your location. Cell tower logs will show you being at a given location. Law enforcement agencies use this capability constantly; they're very good at it.

If you're going to a peaceful event your risk of these things is minimal. When you think there may be troublemakers at the event, or think that authorities will target attendees, consider options like a burner phone (explained in Chapter 4).

The network you'll be using is fully monitored for unencrypted and encrypted communications. If things go sideways, traffic logs by the cellular company (if law enforcement isn't directly engaged at the moment) can and will be used.

Is your device encrypted? iPhones are best for consumers but not impenetrable. As of this writing, everything up to iPhone 6Plus can now be broken into, but I firmly believe the ability to crack future versions will eventually happen.

Worried about losing your media or losing your phone in case of arrest? Set up a way to automatically push your media up to the cloud each time you take a photo or video, which will only work as long as you have reception. Also, back up a copy of all the photos, videos, data, and your address book on your phone before you go— just in case.

Phone prep:

- Secure your device
- Attach a wrist strap
- Sign out of apps you're not using
- Delete everything you can
- Download maps
- Avoid most surveillance with Airplane Mode

Carefully consider how much gear you're bringing, and how you plan to keep track of it. Minimal gear is always best. Wear comfortable shoes and clothes you can move easily in. Bring the minimum amount of stuff to keep your bag or pockets light. Bring extra batteries, storage cards, and your own charger. Pack water, a snack, sunscreen, your ID, and prescriptions you need. Don't bring drugs, booze, explosives, weapons, or anything illegal.

Protest prep:

- Comfortable clothes, layers
- Pack light

- Snacks, water, bandana
- Make a plan in case you lose each other

Additionally, have a pass code or PIN on every piece of digital gear you possibly can, attach wrist straps to everything, and sign out of apps you're not using.

Buddy systems and planning ahead

Formulate a digital strategy with your friends before going. Agree on which encrypted app everyone will be using to communicate, and which sharing sites you're focusing on. Find out if anyone in your group would rather not be in photos or videos.

Cell phone service will be degraded, at the very least because there will be so many people using it. Create a file (in notes, a photo, a text document, or a PDF) that doesn't require you to use the Internet to access it. On this file, put everyone's contact numbers, a phone number for your lawyer or a legal advocacy group, your emergency contact, and a map of the area or building you'll all be in. This way you can get to it when you can't get cell service or Wi-Fi is down.

Before you go, review maps of the area. Make a plan with your friends about where to meet, and where to meet if you get separated. Set a time limit and make your meeting point specific. For instance, if you get separated for more than fifteen minutes, meet at the McDonald's on Market Street. Don't just select a corner, park, street or city block: If you say "the corner of Market and Castro," how will you know which corner in a giant crowd? Landmarks are also easier to find in mass marches when street signs may not be visible. Be sure to plan how you'll end the event; set a time and an area you plan to be in at the finish so you can regroup and decide what to do next.

Before you head out, check to see if any of the people organizing the march or event you're attending has a track record, so you know what to expect. See if their history has any violent or problematic protests. Find out if what you're planning on doing will be in a public, safe space—or not.

It's important to know that in the United States, your First Amendment right to freedom of assembly doesn't mean you can gather anywhere you want. It's meant to limit authorities from infringing on peaceful assembly in public spaces. The problem is, it's often difficult to tell (especially in a city) where the private spaces are in public places; you might wander onto private property that isn't clearly marked without even knowing it. Many seemingly public spaces are owned by corporations; Levi Plaza in San Francisco is just one example. Find out if the place you're going is really a public place—or if it's technically private property.

Such areas are called Privately-Owned Public Space (POPS). You can find them by Googling POPS and the name of your city (also check the POPS entry in this book's "Resources" chapter) and they're often in downtown city office districts. POPS are usually things like small parks, plazas, terraces, or atriums. If you move your protest or assembly into a POPS, and that's when the police can crack down on your protest.

Choose your battles wisely if the police decide to move you anyway. Saying "no" to cops in riot gear is usually a losing proposition, unless your goal is arrest.

How to make the lowest-cost protest sign

Signs and banners send a direct message, and mean your message can be shared across social media or in articles about the event. Some protest signs are funny, others are straightforward, and they range from lipstick on a pizza box to glitter and ribbons. wikiHow and Instructables both have excellent step-by-step guides for making protest signs.

Many marches and rallies don't allow sticks or poles, so you'll need to use sturdy cardboard if you want to have a way to make your sign rise above the crowd. Hollow cardboard tubing, like what you'd pack a poster in to send in the mail, is a good choice in most cases. For the sign itself, cardboard works well, but foamcore is a more resilient choice.

In general, keep your message simple. Look for ideas on Twitter, check out other signs from past marches, and run your idea by a friend or two. Once you've got your slogan, get out the pens or scissors for cutting out construction paper words. Draw your letters out on pieces of paper and arrange them on the sign so you can make sure they'll fit before you commit ink to the board. Know that your main text should be high-contrast to your background so people can easily read it in motion, light, or shadow.

Check your sign for readability by placing it on the other side of a room, and taking a pic of it with your phone.

Foamcore isn't the only way to demonstrate your message. You can create a dynamic, open-source electronic protest sign with a little bit of elbow grease with the instructions in the "Digital Revolutionary Project Guide." This kind of programmable sign can also be tasked with sharing know-your-rights documents, or even placing a phone call in an emergency.

Recording, saving and sharing under stress

Getting perfect photos or video will be a challenge: You'll be moving around a lot, jostled by fellow attendees, dealing with changing light and atmosphere, and under stress. Sometimes you'll need to move just a little, to get the right photo without tripping over your shoelaces. You may need to move a lot if things get weird—up to and including running, jumping, climbing and crawling. Recording and sharing under stress is something that's important to prepare for. There may even be times when you're trying to snap a good picture while taking a risk.

It's critical that you learn how to stay cool under pressure, as well as aware of your surroundings.

Get to know your device better; specifically in the way you'll be using it at the event. You want to be able to get to your photo or video app instantly and take a shot right away. Check your phone (or camera) to make sure it's on an "action" setting, to avoid blur if there's motion. If you can assign a physical button to take photos, do it; you never want to miss the shutter button with your thumb. Practice taking your phone out and grabbing a quick pic. Now try it while walking or going up a flight of stairs.

In a crowd, look around you before taking a photo to make sure you're safe. Be aware of anyone behind you, or others off to the sides. If you're taking a risky photo, be prepared to move in for the shot and back out to get away safely. Always have an exit strategy with shooting photo or video in a sketchy situation. Even better, assign a friend as a "spotter" to grab hold of your belt to pull you back when you need to pay attention (or get away).

During the event, you can take pics or videos of anything in a public space that's in plain view—this includes police and government buildings. Law enforcement can make trouble for you if they've asked you to stop what you're doing and you refuse. They can make even more trouble if they think you're causing a serious threat to public or officer safety. Remember, authorities aren't allowed to see or delete any of your media without a warrant.

How to move and stay safe in a crowd

Big protests and marches like the Women's March on Washington and March for Science happen in the streets because the organizations making them happen get permits beforehand. These permits are for a specific route, date, and time. Outside of this framework, you can peacefully gather and march without a permit when you stay on sidewalks, and you flow in the direction of traffic and pedestrians.

In general, you'll always want to keep the same pace as the crowd you're in and go in the same direction. Make sure your pockets can't be picked, and you haven't left your bag or backpack open while you're walking around.

Going in the same direction as the crowd is even more important if things start to get weird. In this situation, never go against the crowd—even if you have a friend further on in, or lose your buddy. Swimming upstream, or into the push, will get you hurt and not be of any help in getting you where you want to go.

If things get weird:

- Always move with the crowd
- Don't panic
- Pay attention to authorities
- Have a spotter if you document
- Exit the flow on a diagonal

In a situation where people start to rush, panic, or run, always go with the flow, figure out where your exits might be, and get away from the crowd. The danger here is real, and not just from violent police or rabid protesters. Falling down can get you trampled, leaving you injured or worse. You could crushed or have a lot of people fall on top of you, and there's a risk of suffocation because you may not be able to fill your lungs.

People who swim in the ocean, like me, will know how to get out of a riptide—when the ocean pulls you out and away from the coast. When this happens, you swim parallel to the coastline, and it's hard work. You're exhausted afterward, and much further from where you started.

Being in a bad crowd situation is similar. To get out of a scary crowd that's pulling you into its fray, you won't make a sharp right or left turn (cutting across the crowd). Make a gradual right or left across the flow of people, more like a 45-degree diagonal angle. Stay at the speed of the crowd and gradually push through, without panicking or shoving. After you get to "shore," go around a corner. If you can't get fully out yet, get behind a barrier that requires people to go around you. Wait here where you're protected until you see another break in the flow of people, or another opportunity to move.

If you know you're going to a potentially rowdy protest, set up multiple meet-up points, with some being specifically outside of the protest area, and preferably not where the protest may move to. Also maintain situational awareness at all times, and communicate with others to assess out the mood. One problem for people who wanted to get away from the U.C. Berkeley protests was the issue of "police kettling."

"Kettling" is when police corral protestors and anyone inside the zone they want to control. You want to avoid ending up in this zone, but sometimes it's difficult because authorities try to do it without anyone figuring it out. Sometimes they will give warning over a bullhorn and ask to disperse within a certain amount of time. That's when you decide whether the situation is worth potential detention or arrest, or if you're better off leaving to regroup elsewhere.

While in the crowd, you may want to split up with your group intentionally. Always split off with a buddy; never go alone. This way both of you have "eyes and ears" for risk, danger, and maintaining safety when taking photos or video. Have everyone agree to meeting points where you'll check in during the event.

Protests at U.C. Berkeley after the 2016 election were infamous not just because of the clashes between pro-Nazi and anti-fascist groups, but also because of the violence. If there was a conservative speaker booked for the notoriously liberal campus, you could count on the fact that there would be something riotous going on that night. As Berkeley continued to push the envelope with its speaker schedule, the more antagonistic groups were attracted.

Before one event that (predictably) turned violent, Nazi groups communicated their intentions and shared pictures of themselves on social media. One set of photos showed young men camping out on a lawn and posing tough for the camera, waiting for the event with gallon cartons of milk. They had clearly read online that milk is a remedy for chemicals like tear gas or pepper spray. And they were hopeful.

They were also amateurs who hadn't survived direct contact in a riot situation with tear gas or pepper spray. Unless you are wearing a full mask and respirator that doesn't move from your face in any way, if you get hit with chemicals, you're going down. And if the police want you, you're done; if you look to be withstanding the onslaught they'll just do it with overwhelming force (as in, more people and gear and training). Yes, you can use milk to wash it out and reduce the effects, but that requires people to help you and guide you out. This also slows everyone down, and allows them to be gassed and arrested, too.

The smartest thing to do is not put yourself in that situation, or get out before it happens. Most of the time, police tell you they're about to gas or spray you. Not all the time, but police will generally state (via bullhorn or shouting at you) what action they're about to take and what law you're breaking. If police are already grabbing people, then it's already been established that you stand a chance of being gassed.

Potentially riotous crowd situations are a serious thing to prepare for. If this is either your goal or fear, the smartest thing you can do is study an online series called "OPSEC for Activists" by security researcher Elle Armageddon (read parts 1, 2, and 3) and follow the Tumblr of the same name (opsecforactivists.tumblr.com).

Low-cost protective gear

As you've been able to tell, this book is for people who want to show up for justice and make their protests effective, and not really for people who seek out getting beat up by police. Unfortunately, authorities abuse power, and sometimes a peaceful march has a problem. So if you want to wear protective gear, you're not totally nuts.

Most events you attend will be peaceful, but sometimes the unexpected occurs. In May 2017, armed thugs belonging to President Recep Tayyip Erdogan of Turkey violently assaulted American protesters outside the Turkish ambassador's residence, in what the police characterized as "a brutal attack." The peaceful assembly was protesting Erdogan's policies in Turkey, in Syria and in Iraq, as he met with Trump at the White House. Washington D.C. police engaged in physical combat with Erdogan's staff, and Facebook video of the incident showed the officers chasing the thugs away from their victims. Something like this is difficult to predict, but it pays to be cautious.

In demonstrations against Venezuelan President Nicolás Maduro in Caracas on May 3, 2017, clashes between protesters and National Guard troops became frightening and lethal. Demonstrators kitted themselves out in improvised armor and homemade combat gear, which they combined with donated gas masks and helmets. They made shields from wood and scrap metal, gas masks from plastic bottles; they wore goggles, bandanas, and heavy gardening gloves. Some brought spray bottles of antacid to help relieve the burning from tear gas. Venezuelans outside the country shipped in thousands of motorcycle helmets.

The Internet is packed with hilarious how-to's on what gear to wear to a protest. The assumption with these instructionals is that you'll be walking into a complete riot inside a *Mad Max* movie. My favorite is wikiHow, because it's half useful information, and half comedy. If you followed it to the letter, you'd attend the March for Science in a football helmet, protective cup and bad body armor from various athletic groups; you'd have layers of clothes over that, and somehow be wearing a gas mask at the same time. You'd have a hell of a time running.

Wear shoes you can run in. Find cheap, hopefully inconspicuous things like elbow pads and kneepads on eBay. Wear a hat and a bandana around your neck, which you can use to mitigate spray or gas. Leave your contact lenses at home. Wear gloves and safety glasses, and consider wearing a shirt you can leave behind if someone tries to grab you. Above all, you want to be both comfortable and prepared if something bad happens.

Know your rights; if you're arrested

There may come a point, someday, when you find yourself talking to police. It could be when they're just observing a march and ask you to stay on the planned route, or they may be asking you about the event. Conversely, police could be telling you to leave the area immediately. And there may be a time when you end up in a group that's being detained or arrested.

As we've seen with the inauguration protests of 2017, you don't even need to be causing trouble to be arrested in a sweep. You just might be in the wrong place, at the wrong time, with authorities doing something that could be violating your rights. This section is comprised of suggestions and wayfinding information for talking to police, primarily in the United States. It's not a substitute for legal advice. You should absolutely contact an attorney if you've been arrested or think that authorities in any way have violated your rights.

There was a time not so long ago that I was a member of an arts organization that did performances in the street, unannounced, and sometimes with political (but always provocative) themes. Our crew didn't perform; our remote-controlled robots and machines did. When we'd pick a place to show up and do a spontaneous 20 or 30 minute "performance," it would require weeks of advance planning. This was what it took to get our equipment in and out quickly, to plan around the possibility of having our artwork confiscated or crew members detained, and yes—to plan how to clean up our messes.

In the decade-plus that I worked with the group ("Survival Research Laboratories") we'd occasionally have an arrest, or a machine would get held by authorities. In San Francisco, where we were from and where we did most of our performances, the police and fire department got to know us. They didn't like us.

One night we were loading machines and other props into an alley, and a police car pulled in to block the street. I was elected to go talk to them. I walked over to the car as one officer was getting out and said, "Hi. Do you have any questions? We're just loading artwork into the gallery."

The officer paused before speaking. He looked down the alley and back at me, thinking for a moment. He said, "Look, we know who you are."

I replied, "Okay. Well my name is Violet. What can I do for you?"

He sighed. "You have one hour. Keep people off the balconies and rooftops." I repeated his request, agreed, and thanked him. He got in his car and left. When I ran to relay the information, everyone was surprised; we'd thought the event was over before it started. Guess who had the job of talking to police from that point onward? As a result, I've spoken to police while doing dubious things from coast to coast, and in various countries including Berlin (Germany), Lisbon (Portugal), and Tokyo (Japan).

There are things to know before voluntarily speaking with a police officer. Some attorneys say you should never speak to an officer for any reason, ever. That advice is good if you're being held or are under arrest. But if you're not, it looks suspicious. Your goal is to get the police to move on as quickly as possible, so if you act confrontational or like you're hiding something off the bat, you're not going to have a smooth encounter.

One thing is a constant: Politeness, agreeability, and active listening skills can get you out of many sticky situations. Say hello. Try to be calm and centered. Talk to them like you understand they're doing a job; they're either seeking facts or trying to solve a problem. You want to help them solve that problem to the best of your ability. Never, ever say more than you need to.

Practice active listening: This means you repeat what you're hearing someone say in order to clarify and acknowledge what they've said. This accomplishes the neat trick of making someone feel heard, which gets everyone closer to a solution. It moves the discussion toward the police leaving you alone, which is ultimately what everyone wants.

If you think you might be implicated in a crime, keep your mouth shut—even if you're innocent. In the United States you're legally obligated to tell an officer your name and what you're doing at the moment if you're caught doing something suspicious.

Read the ACLU's "Know Your Rights: Stops and Arrests: What to do When Encountering Law Enforcement" booklet. It explains that if you're stopped you don't have to answer any questions. You can politely (and calmly) decline and walk away. Never run from the officer you're talking to. Ask if you are free to go, and if the answer is yes, then you can do so. If they say you're not under arrest but you still can't leave, the ACLU explains that this mean you're being detained. It's not the same, but it may mean an arrest is imminent. According to ACLU, police can, "pat down the outside of your clothing only if they have "reasonable suspicion" (i.e., an objective reason to suspect) that you might be armed and dangerous. If they search any more than this, say clearly, "I do not consent to a search.""

The booklet goes on to explain that in the event they continue to search you after you've said no, that you shouldn't resist them. " You do not need to answer any questions if you are detained or arrested, except that the police may ask for your name once you have been detained, and you can be arrested in some states for refusing to provide it."

Read the ACLU's "Know Your Rights: Stops and Arrests" at least once, and keep a copy on your device. Share it with friends those with whom you attend protests and marches—just in case.

The EFF has a great tip sheet for talking to the police in the event authorities ask to search your electronic devices. You can find a .pdf version of it on their website (eff.org/files/eff_police_tips_2011.pdf). It makes a great addition to your community library (Chapter 6), and the documents you carry with you to events. The tip sheet advises that you don't consent to a search of any kind; this protects you in the United States, though you won't have the same rights to refuse search at borders. You don't have to give police your passwords or your encryption keys, though fingerprint scans (like Touch ID) aren't legally protected like passwords are.

When you can't be there: Digital support

We can't always be there. Most of us have jobs, families, and life's stresses constantly running in the backgrounds of our lives—not all of us can drop everything to be the support for democracy we want to see in the world. Even if we could, we're not all in bodies that can walk, stand, march, or surpass limitations to mobility. None of that can stop us from showing up in a different way.

In the first chapter of this book there's a section called "Seven ways to resist every day." Every single item on that list can be done without leaving the house. They include sharing articles and media, signing online petitions, making donations, and giving emotional support to people who are working hard for positive change.

There is a large and growing arena of opportunity for people who want to participate but can't leave their homes. It's called "microvolunteering," where you perform small tasks for organizations that need stuff done, like tagging photos for organizations that support climate research. The clearinghouse for a wide variety of activities and range of organizations can be found at microvolunteeringday.org.

Amplify. Don't let anyone discourage you from resharing posts and links, or making your act of support simply clicking "Like" or the little heart button on Twitter. There's no shame in "clicktivism" because it works. As we've seen with disinformation campaigns like the one that swayed the US election, these little things add up to shaping perception in a big way. This support is even more important during a march, protest or event. It's one thing to go there and make the media—the people on the ground need an army of supporters at home to get the message out, loud and clear.

CHAPTER 10

RESOURCES

CHAPTER 1: RESIST

Signal Boost:

https://www.theverge.com/2017/1/12/14244634/signal-app-secure-messaging-trump-surveillance-encryption

Digital revolutionary fundamentals

Black Youth Project 100: http://byp100.org/

Chaos Computer Club: https://ccc.de/en/

Dream Defenders: http://dreamdefenders.org/

Electronic Frontier Foundation (EFF): https://eff.org

L0pht: http://www.l0pht.com/

Million Hoodies Movement for Justice: http://millionhoodies.net/

The Women's March: https://womensmarch.com

Identity and keeping things separate

101 Ways I Screwed Up Making a Fake Identity:

https://tisiphone.net/2016/10/13/101-ways-i-screwed-up-making-a-fake-identity/

Domain Games: Role-playing an online identity:

https://exposingtheinvisible.org/resources/watching-out-yourself/domain-games

Hacker OPSEC with The Grugq: https://blogsofwar.com/hacker-opsec-with-the-grugq

Operational Security and the real world: https://grugq.tumblr.com/post/75126493347/operational-security-and-the-real-world

Social Media Self-Defense: http://blog.totallynotmalware.net/?p=15

Technical Anonymity Guide: https://blog.securityevaluators.com/technical-anonymity-guide-658a53adff5b

The Twitter Activist Security: Guidelines for safer resistance: https://medium.com/@thegrugq/twitter-activist-security-7c806bae9cb0

Focus your fight

Black Lives Matter: http://blacklivesmatter.com/

Planned Parenthood: https://plannedparenthood.org

Seven ways to resist every day

ACLU: https://aclu.org

Disconnect: https://disconnect.me

National Lawyers Guild: https://nlg.org

Signal: https://whispersystems.org

WhatsApp: https://whatsapp.com

CHAPTER 2: SELF-CARE RULES EVERYTHING AROUND ME (SCREAM)

Pew Research Center: The Political Environment on Social Media:

http://pewinternet.org/2016/10/25/the-political-environment-on-social-media/

Automation: keep it going when you need a break

Amazon Smile: https://smile.amazon.com/

Daily Action: https://dailyaction.org/

Evernote: https://evernote.com/

Feedly: https://feedly.com

Five Calls: https://5calls.org/

Flipboard: https://flipboard.com/

IFTTT: https://ifttt.com/discover

Instapaper: https://www.instapaper.com

Pinterest: https://www.pinterest.com/

Pocket: https://getpocket.com/

Resistbot: https://resistbot.io/

Tweetdeck: https://tweetdeck.twitter.com/

What the Fuck Just Happened Today?:
https://whatthefuckjusthappenedtoday.com

Groups to join

350: https://350.org/

ActBlue: https://secure.actblue.com/

Commit to Flip: https://commit.flippable.org/

Holy Fuck The Election: http://www.holyfucktheelection.com/

Indivisible Guide: https://www.indivisibleguide.com/

Movement Match: http://jointhemovementtoday.weebly.com/

MoveOn: https://moveon.org

RiseStronger: https://risestronger.org

Swing Left: https://swingleft.org

Town Hall Project: https://townhallproject-86312.firebaseapp.com/

Trumpcare Toolkit: https://trumpcaretoolkit.org/

A List of Pro-Women, Pro-Immigrant, Pro-Earth, Anti-Bigotry Organizations That Need Your Support: http://jezebel.com/a-list-of-pro-women-pro-immigrant-pro-earth-anti-big-1788752078

A Nervous Wreck's Disabled Guide to Stepping Up: https://medium.com/@mahdialynn/a-nervous-wrecks-disabled-guide-to-stepping-up-a6bdc95553b0 - .v4e758817

How to call your reps when you have social anxiety: http://echothroughthefog.cordeliadillon.com/post/153393286626/how-to-call-your-reps-when-you-have-social-anxiety

How to Help Once You're Done Mourning The Election: http://www.complex.com/life/2016/11/organizations-to-donate-to-volunteer-for-post-election

So, you're FIRED UP!? Now what?: http://berc.berkeley.edu/so-youre-fired-up-now-what/

Trust but verify: Poison people

"But he does good work": https://medium.com/@violetblue/but-he-does-good-work-6710df9d9029

Holistic Security: https://holistic-security.tacticaltech.org/

Self-care guidelines

American Counseling Association (counselor and therapist locators): http://counseling.org/

American Psychological Association, Psychology help center:

http://apa.org/helpcenter/

Confidential online counseling, therapy, and assessments:

http://breakthrough.com/

National Association of Social Workers:

http://helpstartshere.org/find-a-social-worker/

National Suicide Prevention Lifeline:

https://suicidepreventionlifeline.org/

Rape, Abuse & Incest National Network: http://rainn.org/get-help/ or 1.800.656.HOPE [4673]

Tech-aware therapists guide:

https://smartprivacy.tumblr.com/therapists

Without My Consent: http://www.withoutmyconsent.org/

Online attacks and trolls

Smart Girl's Guide to Privacy:

https://www.nostarch.com/smartgirlsguide

Speak Up & Stay Safe(r):

https://onlinesafety.feministfrequency.com/en/

Ask: Building Consent Culture, a book by Kitty Stryker

The Smart Girl's Guide to Privacy, a book by Violet Blue

CHAPTER 3: HACK-PROOF YOUR LIFE

LevelUP (trainings for groups): https://www.level-up.cc/

Tech Solidarity: https://techsolidarity.org/resources.html

Tech Solidarity Basics:

https://techsolidarity.org/resources/basic_security.htm

Tech Solidarity for Journalists:
https://techsolidarity.org/resources/journalist_checkup.html

Hack yourself
Delete Me (Abine): https://www.abine.com/deleteme/landing.php

Get your personal info offline
BeenVerified: http://www.beenverified.com/
DOBSearch: https://www.dobsearch.com/
Intelius: http://www.intelius.com/
LexisNexis: http://www.lexisnexis.com/en-us/products/public -
records.page
Spokeo: http://www.spokeo.com/
WhitePages: http://www.whitepages.com

Secure your devices
1Password: https://1password.com/
CoverMe: http://www.coverme.ws/en/faq.html
Digital Self-Defense in the Time of Trump:
https://www.equalitylabs.org/
Hushed: https://hushed.com/
KeePass: http://keepass.info/
LastPass: https://www.lastpass.com/
Let's Get Safe: https://www.letsgetsafe.org

Reduce your attack surface
Brave: https://brave.com/
Chrome: https://www.google.com/chrome/

CrashPlan: https://www.crashplan.com/en-us/
Disconnect: https://disconnect.me/
Firefox: https://www.mozilla.org/en-US/firefox/products/
Lookout: https://www.lookout.com/products/personal
Prey: https://www.preyproject.com/
uBlock Origin: https://chrome.google.com/webstore/detail/ublock-origin/cjpalhdlnbpafiamejdnhcphjbkeiagm?hl=en

CHAPTER 4: YOUR PHONE IS A TRACKING DEVICE

Creepy wireless stalking made easy:
http://hackaday.com/2016/12/04/creepy-wireless-stalking-made-easy/
iOS Forensics - Physical Extraction, Decoding and Analysis From iOS Devices (Cellebrite): http://www.cellebrite.com/Pages/ios-forensics-physical-extraction-decoding-and-analysis-from-ios-devices
Safe Use of Mobile Devices and the Internet:
https://www.ncsc.gov.uk/guidance/safe-use-mobile-devices-and-internet
Stalking a City for Fun and Frivolity:
https://www.youtube.com/watch?v=ubjuWqUE9wQ

The problem with phones at protests

Facebook, Instagram, and Twitter Provided Data Access for a Surveillance Product Marketed to Target Activists of Color:
https://www.aclunc.org/blog/facebook-instagram-and-twitter-provided-data-access-surveillance-product-marketed-target

Inauguration-protest arrests lead to Facebook data prosecution:
https://www.engadget.com/2017/02/10/inauguration-protest-arrests-lead-to-facebook-data-prosecution/
PredPol: http://www.predpol.com/

Phone signal interception
Cell site simulators (EFF): https://www.eff.org/sls/tech/cell-site-simulators
Phone Monitoring (Privacy International):
https://www.privacyinternational.org/node/76
SnoopSnitch: https://opensource.srlabs.de/projects/snoopsnitch
SnoopSnitch app:
https://play.google.com/store/apps/details?id=de.srlabs.snoopsnitch
Stingray (HackADay): https://hackaday.com/tag/stingray/
Text messages warn Ukraine protesters they are 'participants in mass riot': https://www.theguardian.com/world/2014/jan/21/ukraine-unrest-text-messages-protesters-mass-riot

Best phones to protect your data and best practices
Google Project Fi: https://fi.google.com/

Burner phones and apps
CoverMe: http://www.coverme.ws/en/index.html
Burner: https://www.burnerapp.com/
Hushed: https://hushed.com/
Ting: https://ting.com/
Zip SIM: https://zipsim.us/

CHAPTER 5: DEFY SURVEILLANCE

Protection Circle Surveillance Evasion:
https://protectioncircle.org/2016/06/14/surveillance-evasion/
Surveillance Self-Defense (EFF): https://ssd.eff.org/

Encrypted apps
Signal: https://whispersystems.org/
Threema: https://threema.ch/en
WhatsApp: https://www.whatsapp.com/

VPNs and online anonymity
TCPDump: http://www.tcpdump.org/tcpdump_man.html
Wireshark: https://www.wireshark.org/

Find a safe VPN
Black VPN: https://www.blackvpn.com/
Cocoon: https://getcocoon.com/
Freedome: https://www.f-secure.com/en_US/web/home_us/freedome
How To See If Your VPN Is Leaking Your IP Address:
http://lifehacker.com/how-to-see-if-your-vpn-is-leaking-your-ip-address-and-1685180082
Orbot: https://www.torproject.org/docs/android.html.en
Perfect Privacy: https://www.perfect-privacy.com/
TorGuard: https://torguard.net/
Tunnelbear: https://www.tunnelbear.com/
Which VPN Services Take Your Anonymity Seriously?

(TorrentFreak): https://torrentfreak.com/vpn-services-anonymous-review-2017-170304/

Tor is one option
Tor Project: https://www.torproject.org/

Tor browser: https://www.torproject.org/projects/torbrowser.html.en

Tor anonymity tips:

https://www.torproject.org/download/download.html.en - warning

What if I'm paranoid?
Hide My Ass: https://www.hidemyass.com/proxy

Nautilus Wipe: http://wipetools.tuxfamily.org/nautilus-wipe.html

Tails: https://tails.boum.org

Tails setup assistant: https://tails.boum.org/install/index.en.html

Tails warning page:

https://tails.boum.org/doc/about/warning/index.en.html

Encryption and PGP
CryptoParty: https://www.cryptoparty.in/

HTTPS Everywhere: https://www.eff.org/https-everywhere

OpenPGP: http://openpgp.org/

Mailvelope: https://www.mailvelope.com/en/

GPG Suite: https://gpgtools.org/

Off-the-Record (OTR): https://otr.cypherpunks.ca/

Adium: https://adium.im/

Xabber: https://www.xabber.com/

GPG / Mutt / Gmail:

https://gist.github.com/bnagy/8914f712f689cc01c267

CHAPTER 6: GEAR UP

Blueprint for Revolution: How to Use Rice Pudding, Lego Men, and Other Nonviolent Techniques to Galvanize Communities, Overthrow Dictators, or Simply Change the World by Srdja Popovic

Make your own burner phone

Adafruit FONA: https://www.adafruit.com/product/1946

Arduin-o-Phone: https://learn.adafruit.com/arduin-o-phone-arduino-powered-diy-cellphone/overview

FONA cell phone tutorial: https://learn.adafruit.com/adafruit-fona-mini-gsm-gprs-cellular-phone-module

Ting SIM card: https://www.adafruit.com/product/2505

Body cameras, point and shoots

Drift Stealth: https://driftinnovation.com/

Garmin Virb: https://virb.garmin.com/en-US

GoPro: https://gopro.com/

iSAW Edge Lite: https://www.isawcamera.us/isaw-edge-lite

TomTom Bandit: https://www.tomtom.com/en_us/action-camera/action-camera/

Make a tiny wearable time-lapse camera

Tutorial, mini timelapse: https://blog.adafruit.com/2017/02/01/new-project-diy-mini-portable-timelapse-camera

Tutorial, wearable Raspberry Pi:

https://learn.adafruit.com/raspberry-pi-wearable-time-lapse-camera/overview

Batteries and cards

MintyBoost kit: https://www.adafruit.com/product/14

Tutorial: https://learn.adafruit.com/minty-boost

How to make/use a Wi-Fi "library" of resources, rights, maps

Digital Free Library tutorial: https://learn.adafruit.com/digital-free-library/what-youll-need

Raspberry Pi Zero: https://www.adafruit.com/product/3409

Docs to keep with you

ACLU Know Your Rights (index): https://www.aclu.org/know-your-rights

Bill of Rights: http://billofrightsinstitute.org/wp-content/uploads/2011/12/BillofRights.pdf

EFF's Know Your Rights:
https://www.eff.org/files/eff_know_your_rights_2011_0.pdf

Talking to police (know your rights):
http://toasterdog.com/files/KnowYourRightsCards_TheLaw.pdf

U.S. Constitution:
https://constitutioncenter.org/media/files/constitution.pdf

Make an open source protest sign

Adafruit FONA cell phone tutorial: https://learn.adafruit.com/adafruit-fona-mini-gsm-gprs-cellular-phone-module

"An electronic protest sign" tutorial:
https://github.com/brightcolorfulflickers/protestsign

Connecting a 16x32 RGB LED Matrix Panel to a Raspberry Pi:
https://learn.adafruit.com/connecting-a-16x32-rgb-led-matrix-panel-to-a-raspberry-pi/overview

Security gadgets

Fossil: https://www.fossil.com/us/en/search.rfid.html

Onion Pi: https://learn.adafruit.com/onion-pi/overview

PortaPow: http://www.portablepowersupplies.co.uk/

The Lock-Pick Card: https://store.itstactical.com/its-entry-card.html

Tumi: https://www.tumi.com/c/accessories/rfid-wallets-cardcases

YubiKey: https://www.yubico.com/start/

Raspberry Pi User Guide, a book by Eben Upton and Gareth Halfacree

Charlatans and bad activist advice

Security Community Errata: http://attrition.org/errata/

Security Snake Oil: https://securitysnakeoil.org/

CHAPTER 7: FIGHT CENSORSHIP

How they censor you

The Open Net Initiative: https://opennet.net

When governments censor

Blocked UK: https://blocked.org.uk

Great Firewall of China: http://www.greatfirewallofchina.org

Internet Censorship/Amnesty International:
https://www.amnesty.org/en/latest/news/2017/03/fighting-back-

against-cyber-censorship/

Open Rights Group: https://www.openrightsgroup.org/

How Syria Turned Off the Internet: https://blog.cloudflare.com/how-syria-turned-off-the-internet/

The New York Times vs. the 'Great Firewall' of China: https://www.nytimes.com/2017/03/31/insider/the-new-york-times-vs-the-great-firewall-of-china.htmlCommotion Wireless: https://commotionwireless.net

U.S. Underwrites Internet Detour Around Censors Abroad: https://www.nytimes.com/2011/06/12/world/12internet.html

How to use SecureDrop

Federal Employees Guide to Sharing Key Information with the Public: https://lieu.house.gov/federal-employees-guide-sharing-key-information

SecureDrop: https://securedrop.org/

The official SecureDrop Directory: https://securedrop.org/directory

Guardian SecureDrop: https://securedrop.theguardian.com/

Intercept SecureDrop: https://theintercept.com/leak/

New Yorker SecureDrop: https://projects.newyorker.com/strongbox/

New York Times SecureDrop: https://www.nytimes.com/newsgraphics/2016/news-tips/ -securedrop

ProPublica SecureDrop: https://securedrop.propublica.org/

Washington Post SecureDrop: https://www.washingtonpost.com/securedrop/

CHAPTER 8: THE REVOLUTION WILL BE SHARED

James Nachtwey TED Talk:

https://www.ted.com/talks/james_nachtwey_s_searing_pictures_of_war/transcript

Livestreaming concerns

eyeWitness to Atrocities: http://www.eyewitnessproject.org/

CameraV: https://guardianproject.info/apps/camerav/

Mobile Martus: https://www.martus.org/

Obscuracam: https://guardianproject.info/apps/obscuracam/

Video As Evidence: Basic Practices (Witness Blog):

https://blog.witness.org/2015/02/video-as-evidence-basic-practices/

Create memes that matter

Evil Kermit: http://knowyourmeme.com/memes/evil-kermit

Imgflip Meme Generator: https://imgflip.com/memegenerator

Know Your Meme: http://knowyourmeme.com/

Measure your impact

SocDir: http://socdir.com/

Tools for tracking topics and events

Anewstip: https://anewstip.com/

Cyfe: http://www.cyfe.com/

Google Trends: https://trends.google.com/trends/

Hootsuite: https://hootsuite.com/

Mention: https://mention.com/

Social Mention: http://www.socialmention.com/

Top-Hashtags: https://top-hashtags.com/

CHAPTER 9: TAKING IT TO THE STREETS

Ruckus: http://ruckus.org/

How to Protest Without Sacrificing Your Digital Privacy:
https://motherboard.vice.com/en_us/article/guide-protect-digital-privacy-during-protest

Buddy systems and planning ahead

Privately-Owned Public Space (POPS) list:
http://www.metafilter.com/119525/Privately-Owned-Public-Spaces

How to move and stay safe in a crowd

Black Bloc security culture:
https://guerrillanews.wordpress.com/tag/black-bloc/

FEMA Field Force manual offers protesters insights into the future of crowd control (Muckrock):
https://www.muckrock.com/news/archives/2016/dec/13/fema-field-force-manual-offers-protesters-insights/

OPSEC for Activists 1: http://blog.totallynotmalware.net/?p=106

OPSEC for Activists 2 (Packing for a Protest):
https://www.patreon.com/posts/opsec-for-part-2-5218151

OPSEC for Activists 3 (Always Carry A Bandana):
http://blog.totallynotmalware.net/?p=286

OpSec for Activists (Tumblr): https://opsecforactivists.tumblr.com/

Quick and Dirty Tear Gas Primer (Elle Armageddon):
https://www.patreon.com/posts/quick-and-dirty-6057497

Solving the first contact problem: https://tinfoil.press/t/solving-the-first-contact-problem/89/16

Know your rights; if you're arrested

How To Spot Undercover Police:
https://nevergetbusted.com/2012/08/28/spotting-undercovers-article/

Know Your Rights: Stops and Arrests (ACLU):
https://www.aclu.org/know-your-rights/stops-and-arrests-what-do-when-encountering-law-enforcement

Police Tips on Electronic Search (EFF):
https://eff.org/files/eff_police_tips_2011.pdf

When you can't be there: digital support

Micro Volunteering Day: https://microvolunteeringday.com/

CHAPTER 11

THE DIGITAL REVOLUTIONARY PROJECT GUIDE

Just getting started with DIY tech projects? For the fundamentals, check out these great tutorials:

Adafruit Guide to Excellent Soldering: https://learn.adafruit.com/adafruit-guide-excellent-soldering
Super-easy "how to solder" comic: http://mightyohm.com/files/soldercomic/FullSolderComic_EN.pdf
Through-Hole Soldering: https://learn.sparkfun.com/tutorials/how-to-solder-through-hole-soldering

Arduino Setup Guide: https://www.arduino.cc/en/Guide/HomePage
Command Line Crash Course: https://learnpythonthehardway.org/book/appendixa.html
Learn Linux with Raspberry Pi: https://learn.adafruit.com/series/learn-linux-with-raspberry-pi
What is the Command Line? https://learn.adafruit.com/what-is-the-command-line

Digital Free Library
Carry a little device that's a Wi-Fi access point where friends can

browse and download docs that have valuable information and resources.

Original: https://littlefreelibrary.org/

Tutorial: https://learn.adafruit.com/digital-free-library/what-youll-need

Install Apache: https://www.raspberrypi.org/documentation/remote-access/web-server/apache.md

Setting up Raspberry Pi as an access point: https://learn.adafruit.com/setting-up-a-raspberry-pi-as-a-wifi-access-point/overview

Simple website template: https://cdn-learn.adafruit.com/assets/assets/000/037/790/original/digitallibrary.zip?1480980490

DIY Wearable Time Lapse Camera

Hands-free documentation that's unobtrusive. Make a fun video with the photos!

Tutorial, mini timelapse: https://blog.adafruit.com/2017/02/01/new-project-diy-mini-portable-timelapse-camera/

Tutorial, wearable Raspberry Pi: https://learn.adafruit.com/raspberry-pi-wearable-time-lapse-camera/overview

Make Your Own Burner Phone

Minimize your surveillance footprint by making your own "burner" phone.

Adafruit FONA kit: https://www.adafruit.com/product/1946

Arduin-o-Phone: https://learn.adafruit.com/arduin-o-phone-arduino-powered-diy-cellphone/overview

FONA cell phone tutorial: https://learn.adafruit.com/adafruit-fona-mini-gsm-gprs-cellular-phone-module

Ting SIM card: https://www.adafruit.com/product/2505

MintyBoost

A tiny portable battery for anything, that powers your devices for hours. If you want to get started with hardware hacking or any of these projects, the MintyBoost is the perfect place to start.

Starter kit: https://www.adafruit.com/product/14

Tutorial: https://learn.adafruit.com/minty-boost/solder-it

Mobile "graffiti" machine

Put together a Raspberry Pi and a small handheld projector (like a pico projector) to make a great little standalone light 'graffiti' machine. You'll have the Pi boot into an image displaying program (maybe skip the init system entirely and make it PID 1). Find a pico projector that can be powered from 5V so both Pi and projector can be powered from a big USB battery pack.

Raspberry Pi Zero: https://www.adafruit.com/product/3409

Raspberry Pi User Guide, a book by Eben Upton and Gareth

Halfacree

Onion Pi

A small, portable device that runs Tor. Route your Ethernet cable through it for anonymized Internet browsing. Don't forget to change the default password!

Prep: https://learn.adafruit.com/onion-pi/install-tor?view=all - preparation

Tutorial: https://learn.adafruit.com/onion-pi/install-tor

Configure the Pi: http://learn.adafruit.com/adafruits-raspberry-pi-lesson-2-first-time-configuration

Starter kit: http://www.adafruit.com/products/1410

Open Source Protest Sign

Make a glowing sign that lets you change its message, or run several different slogans. Add a Digital Free Library or DIY burner phone to expand its uses.

Connecting a 16x32 RGB LED Matrix Panel to a Raspberry Pi: https://learn.adafruit.com/connecting-a-16x32-rgb-led-matrix-panel-to-a-raspberry-pi/overview

Adafruit FONA cell phone tutorial: https://learn.adafruit.com/adafruit-fona-mini-gsm-gprs-cellular-phone-module

"An electronic protest sign" tutorial: https://github.com/brightcolorfulflickers/protestsign

ACKNOWLEDGEMENTS

This book came from a community.

It happened in January 2017, at a regular drink-up that I host here in San Francisco. On the same day every week, at the same bar, at the same time, no matter if I'm in attendance or not. We call it Hacker Happy Hour, or H3 for short. It's an invitation-only affair, but invitations are pretty easy to come by if you're there for the right reasons. The event warmly welcomes hackers and researchers of all genders and orientations, with firm rules that I laid out a few years ago, and enforce with little mercy.

Those rules are based on trust and a bit of a punk rock attitude. I recite them to all newcomers. No pitches or recruiting, no "rock stars" or groupies, and no drama. We like red teams (hackers hired to attack for the purpose of exposing weaknesses), and controversial attacks. It is not a hackathon or a work event; this is where we relax and talk about our favorite TV shows as much as the latest cool hack or devious attack. No journalists trolling for stories are allowed. Everyone is responsible and accountable for the behavior of the person or people they bring. If anyone sees nonconsensual behavior they're to come get me for intervention. If anyone makes an attendee feel uncomfortable or unsafe, I take care of it—which usually means personally throwing them out.

It's in this environment that *Digital Revolutionary* was born, planned, worked on, and developed with the community of H3—and beyond. Red teams, who break into systems and companies for a living, from the most recognizable companies in the world, left their fingerprints in this book. They are people who want you to resist, and rise up, to fight injustice so strongly that they shared their secrets and allowed me to translate them. My gratitude is fathomless. I can't thank you enough.

You may have noticed a strong tie to indie, open source (and woman-owned) tech company Adafruit throughout this book. Once this book got going, Limor Fried and Phillip Torrone became its champions, and my stalwart supporters in its mission. Adafruit is at the heart of, and behind, sections in this book that it couldn't live without. They reviews they provided, sometimes technical, were invaluable. Their constant support throughout this process and endless faith in me kept me breathing. Since they're also among the people I care about most in the world, I'll be thanking them and celebrating the community and friendship they make me feel for a long time to come.

I have to thank Jamie Zawinski for the direction, criticism and continual help with this book's cover art, and for the camaraderie during the insanity of writing this beast. And the drinks, and listening to me about the book's process, and generally going "WTF" with me at every unbelievable turn of the news about our country going up in flames before our very eyes.

To the hackers who read my manuscript and gave me technical reviews and criticism, or just a hearty "fuck yeah" on the project's details, I am in your debt. Thank you. The chapter on protests required interviews with physical security professionals and hackers who "do physical"—especially ones with experience in riot and "black bloc" conditions. Their input was invaluable, and my gratitude is deep.

I'm indebted to the professionals who spent their time doing technical review on this manuscript: Attorneys, psychologists, security researchers of various specialties, hardware hackers, and more. Thank you especially to security researcher Ben Actis. I don't know where the chapter on poison people and emotional survival would be without the careful review and incredible suggestions from Dr. Keely Kolmes, Psy.D. This is a self-published and very bootstrapped book, and that Dr. Kolmes donated her professional time puts me forever (and happily) in her debt. Thank you.

Have I mentioned that this book comes from a community? It's huge. I had to self-publish this book because I couldn't trust a publisher with it, nor do I have the resources (read: money or privilege) to do the agent-big publisher system. And because of the nature of this book, I had to work with people I trust. That's Thomas S. Roche, my close friend of nearly two decades, one of the best writers I know, and the skilled pro who edited this manuscript. Even when I couldn't stop writing it after he was already working on it. Thank you for being such an incredible editor, and friend. I also want to thank Richard Kadrey for helping me find a proofreader who both "gets it" and is one of the best out there. That's proofreader Nicola Ginzler—thank you.

I wanted to write this book, work with these communities, and have it in your hands sooner. But I'm just a freelance writer for hire, and my finances made it impossible—until I reached out to Patreon supporters and asked for help. This book may not have happened sooner, or later, without the Patreon supporters who helped me every month with a dollar, or twenty, or more. I can't thank you enough: Not just for your financial support, but for the faith you place in me with that donation. You absolutely made this book possible. I will always look at this book and think of you. It's impossible to say what it feels like to be constantly attacked, maligned, and trolled online for my writing and my gender, but then to have made this book from the sheer force of your support. The support of people who care. Thank you.

I come from a very rough and poor background. I don't have blood relatives, and I am not well-off. But it doesn't matter. It's overcome by the fact that you've bought this book and you're reading it. You are the reason I'm still here, dear reader. And for all of this, I thank you deepest and most of all. Keep fighting. Keep resisting. And keep caring about one another, as I do for you.

ABOUT THE AUTHOR

Ms. Violet Blue (tinynibbles.com, @violetblue) is a freelance investigative journalist on hacking and cybercrime, as well as a noted columnist and award-winning author. She has reported for outlets that include *CBS News*, *CNET*, *CNN*, *Engadget*, The *Financial Times*, the *San Francisco Chronicle*, and many others.

Ms. Blue has appeared on *CNN* and *The Oprah Winfrey Show*, among others, and has been interviewed, quoted, and featured in a variety of outlets including *BBC*, *The New York Times*, *Guardian*, *Motherboard*, and *The Wall Street Journal*.

She has authored and edited over three dozen books in eight translations. Her most recent title is *The Smart Girl's Guide to Privacy*, which *ELLE Magazine* called "an illuminating handbook for women."

Blue has presented on privacy, harm reduction, technology, hacking and human sexuality at conferences including ETech, LeWeb, CCC, the Forbes Brand Leadership Conference, plus two Google Tech Talks (among many others). *Guardian* has described Blue as "one of the leading figures in tech writing in the world." She is an advisor to Without My Consent, and a member of the Internet Press Guild. Ms. Blue has been "real named" and blocked on Facebook for the safety of its community since reporting in a 2015 Engadget article on the harmful effects of the company's "authentic names" policies on domestic violence victims and LGBT populations.

Made in the USA
San Bernardino, CA
03 July 2017